Praise for *The Book of Awesome Black Americans*

"*Monique L. Jones is my go-to for witty, bold, and compassionate takes on pop culture. In The Book of Awesome Black Americans, Jones brings her impressive breadth of knowledge and slick style to this well-researched and endlessly exciting collection of Black American stories. The Book of Awesome Black Americans sheds new light on familiar heroes and showcases Black Americans we should be talking about more. Activists and rap stars, abolitionists and pioneers, inventors and scientists surge with life throughout this thrilling and comprehensive work. Read this book! It's awesome.*"

—Jennifer Maritza McCauley, National Endowment for the Arts Fellow and author of *SCAR ON/SCAR OFF*

"The Book of Awesome Black Americans *belongs on every coffee table in America. Monique Jones packs her book with astonishing stories of bravery, grit, and joy. The astonishing anecdotes of overlooked personalities and heroes will ensure you never look at history the same again. Who says history has to be boring?*"

—Li Lai, founder of Mediaversity Reviews

"*Monique Jones digs deep to provide little-known facts and context for a marvelous assemblage of our unsung heroes.*"

—Trey Mangum, contributor to *The Hollywood Reporter*

"*Black history has always been more than one month, more than one chapter in a history book. Monique L. Jones's* Book of Awesome Black Americans *show us that and more. Black people built America, despite being ripped from Africa via the act of global terrorism called the Transatlantic Slave Trade. In her vital and thorough book, Jones writes the history we don't learn in school, the history we need to truly understand the multitudes we contain as Black people. This is a textbook in Black excellence and contribution, and it begins a conversation many are too eager to stifle. Black people's history did not begin in 1619, and our place in this country will continue to evolve for many years to come.*"

—Ashley Jones, recipient of the Rona Jaffe Foundation Writer's Award and author of the award-winning poetry collections *Magic City Gospel* and *dark // thing*

"*Monique Jones strikes the balance of fun and learning with her fantastic debut. The Book of Awesome Black Americans gives us an upbeat but necessary lesson on our unsung heroes.*"

—Joi Childs, brand marketer and film/TV critic

THE BOOK OF

Awesome

BLACK
AMERICANS

THE BOOK OF
Awesome
BLACK
AMERICANS

Scientific Pioneers, Trailblazing Entrepreneurs, Barrier-Breaking Activists and Afro-Futurists

Monique L. Jones

Mango Publishing

<small>CORAL GABLES</small>

The Book of Awesome Black Americans: Scientific Pioneers, Trailblazing Entrepreneurs, Barrier-Breaking Activists and Afro-Futurists

Library of Congress Cataloging
ISBN: (p) 978-1-64250-147-6 (e) 978-1-64250-148-3

BISAC: YAN038110, YOUNG ADULT NONFICTION / People & Places / United States / African American

LCCN: 2019948836

Printed in the United States of America

Please note some names have been changed to protect the privacy of individuals.

To everyone important in my life; you know who you are.

To W.E.B. DuBois who came up with the idea for an encyclopedia of African diasporic excellence. To Henry Louis Gates Jr. and Kwame Anthony Appiah for following through with that idea by creating Africana: The Encyclopedia of the African and African-American Experience. *Your work inspired and educated me as a child, and I hope this book passes on that same spirit of learning and pride.*

Table of Contents

THE BOOK OF

Awesome

BLACK
AMERICANS

Introduction

Black history. It's a topic the country revisits every February. But Black history means more than just a cursory look at Black notables during Black History Month. Black History is part of American history. It's important all year round—every second of every day.

The Book of Awesome Black Americans is a look at some of the people who have made this country—and the world—greater by defying the odds, pushing through adversity, and paving a path for others to follow. This book is also a reflection of my own childhood, which was spent researching and reading about Black leaders, inventors, and innovators who shaped how I viewed myself and my place in the world. While this book is just a pittance of the debt they're owed, I hope that it serves as my recognition for the incredible lives they've lived.

There are some things we need to get out of the way before we dive headfirst into this book together. Most of us already know about Martin Luther King Jr., Malcolm X, Rosa Parks, and the like. Indeed, a few folks we always learn about will be included here. But this book is largely dedicated toward those faces and stories we don't see or hear about a lot in the mainstream. This includes LGBTQ+ voices and the voices of people who lived in a time when their stories were considered unimportant. This includes individuals who predate the African American experience, such as the African nobles who are the genesis of African American history. This also includes everyday people past and present who have worked behind the scenes to make our lives, and our futures, better and brighter; they might have gotten accolades for their work, but, if you met them on the street, you probably wouldn't recognize them. Those are the individuals this book is highlighting.

Another thing to note is that I use "Black American" in two different ways in the book. The first way is to discuss African American people, people who are descended from African slaves brought to America. The second way is to write about people from the diaspora who are of African descent but are American citizens. This is because there are some people in the book who might not be descendants of slaves in the United States, but they are, indeed, American citizens of an African background.

I hope that you, the reader, have fun with this book. As a child who loved learning, I was entranced by *Africana*, an encyclopedia set comprised solely of Black American accomplishments, historical dates, and facts written by W.E.B. DuBois and later edited by Henry Louis Gates Jr. and Kwame Anthony Appiah. Through *Africana*, which I read when it was in its website form, I was transported through time and learned so much about my own African American history. Of course, the book you're reading now isn't an encyclopedia. Still, my wish is that it engenders the same type of curiosity and love for learning as *Africana* did for me. I hope that you are inspired to learn more about the people highlighted in this book. I want it to inspire you to go on your own personal, enlightening journey.

(Also, you'll hear a lot about Alabama in this book, since that's where I'm from!)

I hope this book accomplishes its goal of showcasing how vast Black history actually is, particularly Black American history. We live in it every day, whether we realize it or not. It's time to start showing honor to those who have provided us with so much. One of the best ways to do that is to start learning about their impact on our lives.

THE BOOK OF
Awesome
BLACK
AMERICANS

In the Beginning

As with all good stories, we must start at the beginning.
When it comes to Black American history, that story
doesn't start with slavery. Instead, we must go *all* the
way back to where civilization as we know it began:
Africa.

African Roots

If we're starting from the beginning, let's make it
count by starting with the first humans ever. Yes,
African history actually encompasses *all* of human
history, because the first hominins actually arose from
Africa. So, regardless of our ethnicity or nationality,
we all have much more in common than we've made
ourselves believe.

The most famous hominin ancestor is **"Lucy,"** the
nickname for AL 288-1. She's the female skeleton from
the hominin species *Australopithecus afarensis* and
was discovered in the Afar Triangle in Ethiopia in 1974.
While we know her as Lucy, she also has another name,
the Amharic "Dinkinesh." Dinkinesh means "you are
marvelous," and she certainly is, seeing how she holds
some of the answers to human evolution.

Another ancient skeleton—**"Little Foot"**—was
discovered in a South African cave in 1994. Whereas

Lucy was dated as being 3.2 million years old, Little Foot was dated as being about 3.7 million years old, several hundred thousand years older than Lucy.

More recently, others born in the same land became inspiring leaders, generals, royalty, and adventurers rivaling the likes of the Roman and British Empires we are always taught about in schools. Of course, you have Egypt's ancient rulers, the pharaohs. One cool pharaoh is Amenhotep IV, who renamed himself **Akhenaton** after establishing something no other Egyptian ruler had done—a monotheistic religion. This religion was based around Aten, the god of the sun. Even though Akhenaton's monotheistic religion was abolished with the crowning of his son **Tutankhamun** (otherwise known to us as "King Tut," the teenage pharaoh), his contribution to religion affected the practice of worship for world religions for hundreds of years to come.

The Kushites, who lived in current day Sudan, came to power in Egypt when the Kushite **King Piankhi**, also known as Piye, and his brother **King Shabaka** staged a successful coup and established Egypt's twenty-fifth ruling dynasty with King Piankhi's son, **Pharaoh Shebitku** and Shebitku's brother **Taharqa**.

Even though the Egyptians eventually regained their dominance over their region, Nubia cranked out exceptional leaders, like **Queen Amanirenas**, a battle-tested queen who lost an eye in her conquests. She successfully waged an extended war against the Romans occupying her land. Her battle strategy led her to victory against Roman emperor Caesar Augustus, who not only ordered his troops to retreat, but canceled Rome's demand for Kushite tribute.

Another warrior-queen was **Queen Aminatu** of Nigeria. Born in 1533, she was the daughter of **Queen Bakwa Turunku** and inherited her mother's throne in 1576. Aminatu was known for her military might and was able to expand Hausa territory with each of her campaigns. She conquered the neighboring Nupe and Kwararafa states as she expanded her nation. She also succeeded in securing the trade route under Zazzau control, bringing Zazzau even more power. Her reign was the closest any ruler has come to unifying Nigeria under the power of one person.

Mansa Musa was the tenth *Mansa* or "sultan" of the Mali Empire. Musa is known as one of the richest people in all of history, reigning over a kingdom that is thought to have possibly been one of the largest producers of gold in the world. His wealth was documented throughout history, including in a 1375 Catalan Atlas, which depicts him holding a gold coin. This gold coin represented unfathomable riches, which he displayed throughout his pilgrimage to Mecca. It's been recorded that his retinue consisted of sixty thousand men dressed in Persian silk and brocade. Of these, twelve thousand were slaves, carrying four pounds of gold bars each. The procession also included expensively dressed heralds wielding gold staffs and animals including horses and camels, the latter of which carried 50 to 300 pounds of gold dust. Even though Musa was, of course, flexing on those he passed by, the flex was supposedly for a good cause; Musa reportedly gave his gold away to the poor he met while on his trip. His wealth also allowed him to build a mosque every Friday of his journey, spreading the message of Islam while letting folks know he was on an economic level other rulers could only dream of.

Even more incredibly, Musa managed to buy back all of the gold he gave away, after realizing that his acts of charity devalued the price of metals in the cities he visited. So, on the way back from Mecca, he borrowed as much gold as possible from Cairo's brokers. While hard to believe, Musa was indeed able to recover all of the gold he gave away. On top of that, he did it all in the same trip to Mecca. That legendary trip makes him the only man in recorded time to control the price of gold in the Mediterranean region. Wall Street and its brokers have nothing on the likes of this leader.

Askia Mohammad I, also known as Muhammad Ture or Askia the Great, was an emperor of the Songhai Empire. Born in Futa Tooro near Senegal and Mauritania in 1443, Askia's rule consolidated the varying regions of the empire until the Songhai Empire became one of the richest in Africa. Like Mansa Musa, Askia traveled to Mecca with a retinue. His consisted of 500 horsemen and 300,000 pieces of gold. During that trip, Askia met the Caliph of Egypt and, through that meeting, returned with a new title: the Caliph of the Western Sudan, meaning he was the spiritual leader of all Muslims in West Africa. Askia expanded his kingdom to the Hausa in Nigeria and established the Malian city of Timbuktu as one of the world's foremost areas for education and commerce. Under Askia, the Songhai region expanded to the size of the continental US.

● ● ● ● ●

The number of interesting characters in Africa's history pre-slavery could fill up volumes of books or populate movie theaters with Marvel-esque film franchises. Unfortunately, a lot of this history has gone unrecognized by the Western world in large part due to the Transatlantic Slave Trade, which involved the kidnapping and trafficking of millions of Africans from their homes to the New World. It's estimated that 12.5 million captives were brought from Africa to the Americas between 1525 and 1866. That means families were forever broken, knowledge was lost, and communities were deprived of parts of their identities.

It's worth noting that some of the entries in this section include enslaved African Americans who differ in opinion about their treatment in slavery. As you'll read, some actually liked their owners, whereas several more disliked their masters. The differences in opinion must be put in context; some who speak of less-than-horrific experiences can only do so because they happened to have owners who were kinder than most. These types of masters, however, were the exception, and the overarching effect on slavery in the US perpetuated a system of racism that is so entrenched, we still feel its effects today.

Some slaves' gentler accounts also have to do with the wealth and status they had before becoming enslaved. Some of the following slaves were royals in their countries of origin. As such, they might believe they were enslaved because they were wrongly thought of as being part of a lower class, not just because they were Black. As you'll read, one formerly enslaved man even became a slave trader once he was freed and was able to return to Africa.

With that said, every slave listed below has a history that we should learn from. Regardless of their personal stances, their narratives and experiences have helped America move forward toward a more just society.

Transatlantic Survivors

Enslaved Black Americans were faced with hardship and abuse simply because of their skin. Incredibly, many were able to rise above adversity and accomplish great feats. One of those Black Americans who rose to notoriety during slavery's grip on the country was **Abdulrahman Ibrahim ibn Sori**.

Sori was a prince of Fouta Djallon in Guinea and, with a command of two thousand men, was responsible for protecting Guinea's coast and economic interests when he was captured in 1788 and enslaved in the US for forty years. His title of "Prince" became a source of petty humor for those who couldn't believe a Black man could be royalty. Sori's enslavement brought him to Natchez, Mississippi, and, after realizing escape was impossible, he set about earning his freedom by becoming an integral part of the life of his new master, the uneducated Thomas Foster. Thanks to Sori's knowledge of cotton, a native crop of his home country, Foster became one of the South's largest cotton producers. As for Sori, his power earned him limited freedom on the plantation, which allowed him to grow and sell his own vegetables.

After gaining relative freedom and building a family with his wife, Foster's midwife Isabella, Sori was recognized by a random traveler, British surgeon John Cox. Decades before, Sori and his family had helped Cox when he was shipwrecked off the coast of Guinea. Intent on paying Sori back for his kindness, Cox made it his duty to spend the rest of his life buying back Sori's freedom. Even though the surgeon's efforts didn't pan out, Sori became a celebrity due to the story, and he used his status, as well as the country's racism, for his own advantage: he allowed America to believe he was a Moroccan citizen who was wrongly captured.

Morocco was considered different from the remainder of Africa (including West Africa, where many slaves were from). Why was America so friendly with Morocco? Because the Moroccan government was one of the first nations to recognize the US as an independent nation in the late 1700s. Sultan Sidi Muhammad Ben Abdullah extended the proverbial olive branch to create an alliance with America to establish peaceful trade. This explains why Sori felt it was in his best interest to pretend to be Moroccan; if America believed the lie, they would fear ruining trade relations—and Sori would be set free. The almighty dollar is often more powerful to the corrupt than actual human decency.

And so, out of fear of worsening the country's relationship with Morocco, Secretary of State Henry Clay ordered for Sori's release.

His battle to earn the release of his children proved unfruitful, and, even though he did make it to Africa— he arrived in Monrovia after his decades-long battle to return home—he died at age sixty-seven, after contracting a fever from his journey. Tragically, he never reached his homeland or saw his children again.

Thomas Peters was born Thomas Potters and was rumored to have been an African royal kidnapped and enslaved in North Carolina, but little did anyone know that he would become a founding father of an African country. Enlisted as a Black Loyalist in the Black Company of Pioneers, Peters fled his enslavement with the British during the Revolutionary War. When he arrived in Nova Scotia, Canada, he also became notable for his recruitment of Black settlers in the Canadian province to join him in establishing a colony for free Blacks in Sierra Leone, Africa, called Freetown. Freetown is now the largest city and capital of Sierra Leone.

Absalom Jones, born enslaved, founded the African Methodist Episcopal Church (AME), a denomination that is immensely popular today, with seven thousand congregations and a membership of at least 2.5 million. Jones was born into slavery in Sussex County, Delaware, and asked for help to learn how to read. With this education, his owner Benjamin Wynkoop brought him to Philadelphia to serve as a clerk and handyman in a retail store. This allowed Jones to work for himself and keep his pay. During his time as a clerk, he also attended a Quaker-run school, where he learned writing and math.

His earnings allowed him to purchase the freedom of his wife, Mary Thomas, in 1770, and he eventually earned his own freedom through manumission. During his life, he became a businessman owning several properties, and he also organized the Free African Society with his friend Richard Allen. The organization helped those in need, such as orphans, the infirm, widows, and those who needed help with burial expenses. The two were pastors and, because of their charitable efforts, increased their congregation to the point that they were able to create "The African Church," an offshoot of the Free African Society.

Archer Alexander was a former slave who is immortalized in the Emancipation Memorial at St. Louis's Lincoln Park. He was born into slavery in Virginia and was moved to St. Louis with his master before he was sold to another master in Missouri. He eventually became a source of information to Union troops before the Civil War, warning them that a train trestle they were looking to use was sabotaged by Confederate sympathizers. Suspected as the leak, slavers caught up with him, but he broke free and managed to escape back to St. Louis.

He became a part of writer Greenleaf Eliot's life after his wife hired Alexander as a servant. Eliot's personal credo said he wouldn't return a fugitive slave to a former master, so he managed to keep Alexander safe until Lincoln issued the Emancipation Proclamation, allowing him, his wife Louisa, and one of their daughters, Nellie, to be reunited shortly before Louisa's death. Alexander later remarried, but she, too, died one year before Alexander's death in 1880.

While Alexander was alive, his life story as a Union spy compelled Eliot to write his biography, *The Story of Archer Alexander: From Slavery to Freedom*. Sculptor Thomas Ball also utilized Alexander's visage as a model for the freed slave in the Emancipation Memorial. Here's the story of how Alexander became the model: The Western Sanitary Commission, which helped victims of the Civil War, began a fundraising campaign to build a statue after a freed woman gave them five dollars toward building a monument to President Abraham Lincoln. As a person affiliated with the group, Eliot met with Ball about the sculpture. At the meeting, Eliot gave Ball photographs of Alexander to use, because one of the Commission's contingencies was that the statue feature a real freed slave. The statue, which features a freed slave kneeling in gratitude to President Abraham Lincoln, made its debut in 1876.

Alexander also has another connection to today's culture. According to DNA, Alexander's great-granddaughter is the paternal grandmother of "The Greatest," boxer Muhammad Ali. Ironically enough, author Greenleaf Eliot also has a connection; he is the grandfather of famous playwright and poet (and the person we have to blame for *Cats*), T.S. Eliot.

Ayuba Suleiman Diallo was a prominent merchant from Senegal before he and his translator were captured by Mandinka slave traders in 1729 and brought to Maryland. Diallo was eventually freed after his owner was convinced of his nobility by Rev. Thomas Bluett and a letter Diallo wrote to his father. This letter had caught the attention of James Oglethorpe, the director of the business that captured Diallo, the Royal African Company. After his freedom, he was brought to London and became part of the region's elite circle. In a dark twist, he himself became an interpreter and slave trader for the Royal African Company until his death in 1773. Even though he sent fellow Africans to harsh fates, his account of slavery, published by Bluett, is considered vital in understanding the horrific nature of the slave trade.

Dred Scott is the man behind the famous case *Dred Scott v. Sanford*.

As we know, the Dred Scott case involves Scott, an enslaved man, suing for his freedom as well as that of his family. In the suit, he asserts that he, his wife, and his family were free after having lived in the free state of Illinois with his owner before returning to the slave state of Missouri and then completing the journey in the free Wisconsin territory. However, the case has a longer history than what we are taught in the schoolbooks.

Scott was an enslaved man who was owned by John Emerson and his family. It's the Emersons' move between Missouri and Illinois due to John Emerson's military duty that is the basis for Scott's case. But reportedly, after his owner John died, Scott attempted to purchase his freedom from Emerson's widow. She refused, compelling Scott and his lawyers to file individual suits for Scott and his wife, Harriet. The courts in St. Louis agreed that the case should move forward, and, by 1850, Scott had actually won his case on a state level. But the verdict was reversed in 1852 by the Missouri Supreme Court, which invalidated the state's "once free, always free" doctrine.

By this time, Emerson's widow had given estate control to her brother, John F.A. Sanford. Sanford was a New York resident, and, since he wasn't bound by Missouri law, Scott's lawyers filed a case against Sanford in US District Court. Even though the court ruled in Sanford's favor, the case advanced to the Supreme Court.

Unfortunately, the case failed, with the US Supreme Court ruling that no Black person could claim US citizenship nor could they petition for their freedom. Particularly, the ruling made by the majority and written by Chief Justice Roger B. Taney, hinged on the Fifth Amendment, which declares it unconstitutional to be held for a crime barring a correct indictment by police. Slaves, it was argued, are property and therefore not American citizens. As non-citizens, slaves also had no ground to sue for their freedom in court.

Overall, Taney's ruling was a backward attempt to keep racial prejudices intact; his opinion did state that Black people could be citizens and even vote in certain states. But in his view, state citizenship wasn't equal to national citizenship. However, if you're a citizen of a state, you're thereby a citizen of the *United* States. But Taney claimed that while Scott might have been free in one state, he wasn't free in Missouri, where he resided. Ironically, Scott and his family were emancipated merely three months after the Supreme Court decision. Their freedom was granted by the Blow family, who had sold the Scotts to the Emersons in the first place. Scott lived the rest of his life working as a hotel porter in St. Louis, and Harriett worked as a laundress. Unfortunately, Scott died just a little over a year after gaining his hard-fought freedom in 1858. His cause of death was tuberculosis. Incredibly, the Blow family continued to care for Scott after his death, giving him a proper burial.

Scott wasn't the only person in American history to sue for freedom. Hundreds of slaves waged such lawsuits before the Civil War, and **Elizabeth Key Grinstead** is one of those litigious enslaved Americans. She became one of the first Black people in the North American colonies to successfully sue for her freedom. The lawsuit, filed in 1656 in Virginia, was for her freedom as well as the freedom of her infant son. Similarly, **Elizabeth Freeman** successfully sued to be freed by her owners Colonel John Ashley, the judge of the Berkshire Court of Common Pleas, and his wife. Freeman and her sister were wedding presents, in fact, since Ashley's new wife was the daughter of Freeman's former master, Pieter Hogeboom. The newly minted Mrs. Ashley was a cruel mistress to Elizabeth, known as "Mum Bett," and her sister. For instance, when Elizabeth tried to protect her sister from one of Mrs. Ashley's strikes, Elizabeth received a wound on her arm that never healed. Instead of shielding it, she instead kept it visible so everyone could see her mistress's cruelty.

It is Colonel Ashley's own words that gave Elizabeth the keys to the freedom she so desperately wanted. Colonel Ashley was part of the committee that wrote the Sheffield Declaration in 1773, stating that "mankind in a state of nature are equal, free, and independent of each other, and have a right to the undisturbed enjoyment of their lives, their liberty and property." These words compelled Freeman to seek lawyer Theodore Sedgwick for help. In 1781, she actually won her case in the Berkshire Court of Common Pleas, but Ashley refused to release Freeman. That August, the case, *Brom and Bett v. Ashley*, went to the County Court of Common Pleas of Great Barrington, where Sedgwick argued that Massachusetts actually outlawed slavery per the state's constitution. The jury sided with Sedgwick and, finally, Freeman was a free woman. Freeman used her liberty to become a healer, nurse, and midwife. She also worked as a paid domestic to Sedgwick and his second wife, Pamela. Within the home, she became a rock for the family, even helping Pamela through her severe depression. She bought her own house to live with her children. By the time she died in 1829, she had a lineage of grandchildren and great-grandchildren to carry on her legacy.

Interestingly enough, the "Brom" included in the case was the name of another slave, a man named **Brom** who was also a slave in the area. It's unknown as to how he became involved in the case, but it's believed that Brom was also in Ashley's household. At any rate, the case also allowed for Brom's freedom. However, we don't know what became of him. Let's hope he had a better life than the one he led before the case.

Enslaved people also made their way into high office. **Elizabeth Hobbs Keckley** was a former Virginia slave who bought her and her son's freedom in 1855 and eventually became the personal modiste (a personal stylist and dressmaker) and confidante for the First Lady Mary Todd Lincoln. She also became a civil activist and author, who published her memoirs on living in the White House called *Behind the Scenes, Or, Thirty Years a Slave and Four Years in the White House*. While in the White House, Keckley and Fredrick Douglass organized educational programs and relief initiatives for emancipated slaves.

Archibald Grimké was the son of slave Nancy Weston and her owner Henry Grimké in Charleston, North Carolina, but went on to become a founding member of the National Association for the Advancement of Colored People (NAACP).

Archibald and his brother Francis lived as free Black men before his half-brother, Montague, employed them as servants. After suffering abuse at the hands of Montague, he escaped and hid with relatives until Charleston surrendered to the Union during the Civil War.

After attending Lincoln College in Pennsylvania, Grimké became one of the first African American students at Harvard Law School in Massachusetts, later establishing a Boston-based law firm. He also acted as consul to Santo Domingo (the Dominican Republic) and, in 1903, he became the president of the American

Negro Academy until 1919. He helped found the NAACP in 1909 and became the president of the Washington, DC, chapter in 1913. In 1919, he was given the NAACP's highest honor, the Spingarn Medal. Grimké died in 1930.

Estevanico, who was also known as Esteban the Moor, Esteban de Dorantes, Estebanico, or Mustafa Azemmouri, is believed to be one of the first Africans to reach the continental United States. As a boy, he was enslaved by the Portuguese and later sold to a Spanish nobleman. He was aboard the Spanish Narváez expedition to establish a colony in Florida in 1527. He was among the few to survive the trek through Florida, with many of the three hundred men dying along the way from attacks by Florida's Native Americans and the state's harsh jungle. The survivors made barges and tried to sail away to Mexico, but only eighty people survived after the boats capsized near Galveston, Texas. The Native Americans in Texas were friendly at the outset, but eventually enslaved the remaining explorers, and, after five years, only four of the eighty survived, including Estevanico.

Estevanico became an explorer of the American Southwest, traveling with Álvar Núñez Cabeza de Vaca, Andrés Dorantes de Carranza, and Alonso del Castillo Maldonado, the remaining survivors, through New Spain (what is now the US Southwest and northern Mexico) to Mexico City to meet up with Spanish forces. Estevanico and the other survivors became medicine men after living with another Native American tribe, and the four men became known as healers, earning the nickname "The Children of the Sun." Estevanico also became fluent in several Native languages.

Estevanico led a reconnaissance party back through the Southwest for the viceroy of Mexico. But it's believed he was killed by the Zuni in their city of Hawikuh in 1539 because his trademark medicine gourd was trimmed with owl feathers, a bird that's thought to be a symbol of death to the Zuni.

Harriet Ann Jacobs escaped from slavery to protect herself from sexual threats put forth by her owner's father, Dr. James Norcom. She lived as a fugitive for ten years before she was freed by Cornielia Grinnell Willis, the second wife of her employer, poet and editor Nathaniel Parker Willis. She became an abolitionist and an author, writing her autobiography *Incidents in the Life of a Slave Girl,* which included the sexual trauma she and other Black female slaves experienced from their masters. Unfortunately, the book would fall from the public eye until the 1960s and 1970s, when the civil rights movement and women's movement gained traction.

Hannah Crafts, also known as Hannah Bond, is the author of *The Bondwoman's Narrative*, thought to be the first novel by an African American woman, as well as the only one written by a fugitive slave woman. The novel was written in the late 1850s but was only rediscovered and published in 2002 after Harvard professor Henry Lewis Gates Jr. purchased the manuscript.

The slave "Fed" renamed himself **John Brown** and became an author with his book of memoirs, *Slave*

Life in Georgia: A Narrative of the Life, Sufferings, and Escape of John Brown, a Fugitive Slave, Now in England. The book, which was published in London in 1855, contained the dictated accounts of Brown (written by the secretary of the British and Foreign Anti-Slavery Society's secretary, Louis Alexis Chamerovzow) and how he managed to escape from Georgia to England. His memories include abuse, loss, familial separation, medical experimentation, and more. Brown eventually lived a full life in London, marrying a local woman and working as an herbalist. He died in 1876.

Jordan Winston Early was born as a slave in 1814 in Virginia and lived with his maternal aunt, an astronomy-loving uncle, and an older woman known as "Aunt Milly" on his plantation before he became a minister at the young age of twelve. When he and his family were taken to Missouri by their masters in 1826, he was emancipated and began his journey toward becoming an African Methodist Episcopal Church preacher in 1836. After expanding the AME Church in St. Louis, Illinois, Indiana, New Orleans, and Tennessee, Early became a deacon in 1838 and established the first AME Church in St. Louis in 1840.

Jupiter Hammon is known as the first African American poet to be published in America. Born into slavery in New York on Henry Lloyd's estate, Hammon was educated along with his master's children and worked with his master at his businesses. His first work, *An Evening Thought*, also known as *An Evening Prayer* and *An Evening's Thought: Salvation by Christ, with Penitential Cries*, was published in 1760 and used to preach to Lloyd's slaves. In 1787, he spoke to New

York's Black community at the African Society of New York City called "An Address to the Negroes in the State of New York." Despite his celebrity status, Hammon was never freed. He was buried in an unmarked grave on his master's estate.

Lewis Adams, formerly a slave in Alabama, took his passion for education to found the Tuskegee Institute, now known as Tuskegee University, one of the prominent HBCUs in America. Born in 1852, Adams became proficient in reading and writing and became a polyglot even though he had no formal education. He was a Jack of all trades as an expert in tin-smithing, shoe-making, and harness-making. His Tuskegee Institute, which opened in 1881 as the Tuskegee State Normal School, came at the right time for freed Blacks after the Civil War and during Reconstruction, when Black people were in need of gaining different skills to make a living. To show just how interconnected Black leaders were throughout history, the first principal of the Tuskegee Institute was none other than scholar Booker T. Washington.

Omar ibn Said was a wealthy Senegalese Islamic scholar and writer who was captured and enslaved in 1807 in North Carolina. Even though he was never able to return to his Senegalese home of Futa Tooro, Said became an author in the US, writing a series of books on theology and history and an autobiography that was published after his death in 1864. His account of his life in America includes escaping from his first owner, an abusive man named Johnson. He was put in jail and was later recovered by North Carolina governor John Owen and his brother Jim, whom Said described as godly people. He converted to Christianity and remained with his owner's family until his death.

Paul Jennings was a slave who served President James Madison and his family in the Madison family home of Montpelier and in the White House. Jennings' memoir, *A Colored Man's Reminiscences of James Madison*, is thought to be the first memoir about life at the White House. It also provided one of many written accounts of how slaves interacted with their owners, particularly those whose morals seem antithetical to the tenet of slavery. Jennings was later able to buy his freedom via statesman Daniel Webster, and, after gaining his freedom and making a living as a "laborer" by completing clerical tasks, he visited Madison's widow, Dolley Madison, now broke, and provided "small sums of money from [his] own pocket" if he thought she needed it.

Solomon Northup is known to us today because of Chiwetel Ejiofor's dramatic performance in *Twelve Years a Slave*. Of course, like in any film, Northup's account is dramatized for effect. That doesn't mean that the horrors Northup lived through were any less vile or terrifying. The real man behind the film character was an abolitionist, professional violinist, and landowner in New York. Northup was born free as the son of a freed slave and a free woman but was later held hostage in slavery for twelve years, living through unthinkable conditions. His account of his enslavement furthered the abolitionist case in the US and fueled Northup's work with the Underground Railroad as well as his lectures throughout the country. In fact, many freed Black people were kidnapped into slavery, so much so that the exact number of victims is unknown. Sadly, many didn't have the happier fate of Northup, who managed to escape. Many who were sold back into slavery were never heard from again because of the nefarious ways their histories as free individuals were erased. In many instances, their freedom papers were either destroyed or dismissed by judges as being forged, White witnesses refused to testify against their neighbors who were committing these crimes, and much more.

Slavery was much easier to excuse by the masses before the image of **Gordon**, who became known as "Whipped Peter," circulated throughout the nation. Gordon's influential status was established in 1863 after he came to a Union encampment in Baton Rouge. His harrowing escape was just part of the violence he had endured as a slave, which included being whipped nearly to death. The photograph of his raised scars, which traveled the length of his back and were accumulated over years, were revealed during a medical examination and became one of the most widely circulated photographs about slavery at the time, strengthening the abolitionist movement and putting the importance of the Civil War into perspective; as much as the argument could be made about the war being about "economics," it was clear that there were human rights at stake. His photo propelled other Black abolitionist leaders, like Frederick Douglass and Sojourner Truth, to either pose for pictures for circulation or sell them to raise awareness and funds for abolitionist initiatives.

The Bridge to Freedom

Incredibly, there were also enslaved people who lived long enough to not only be emancipated, but to also make headlines in the mid-1900s. **Cudjo Lewis** and **Redoshi** are two of the last slaves to be trafficked across the Atlantic, coming from Africa to Alabama via the *Clotilda*, the last slave ship in operation in the Americas. Cudjo Lewis (born as Oluale Kossola) and Redoshi (also known in the US as Sally Lewis), were both born in Benin and kidnapped into slavery in 1860. Lewis and other *Clotilda* survivors went on to establish Africatown near Mobile, an isolated community of independent freed Blacks who not only shielded themselves from outside discrimination but preserved their shared African culture.

Eliza Moore was also one of the last documented slaves in the Unites States. Moore was born in Montgomery County, Alabama, in 1843 and was a slave to a man named Dr. Taylor. She lived at Gilchrist Place, where she and her husband were sharecroppers for between sixty-five and seventy years. At the time of her death in 1948 at the age of 105, she was thought to be one of Montgomery County's oldest residents, if not the oldest resident. However, her husband was just as blessed with longevity as she was. Ashbury died in 1943, and he too was over a hundred years old.

North Carolina's last Confederate Civil War veteran to receive a Class B pension from the state was **Alfred "Teen" Blackburn**, the last living person in North Carolina's Yadkin County to be counted as a slave.

Similarly to Lewis, Redoshi, and Moore, Blackburn is also one of the last living survivors of slavery in the nation to remember slavery as an adult.

According to his family's accounts, Blackburn was the son of Fannie Blackburn, a biracial Cherokee-African enslaved by Augustus Blackburn, a plantation owner and Confederate colonel in the Civil War. During the Civil War, he served as Augustus's "body servant" and served Blackburn's regiment as the cook and help.

His time after the war included various jobs such as farming, working for a local sheriff, and becoming a contract male carrier for the US Postal Service, where he supervised both White and Black workers for sixty years. He also married a well-to-do White woman named Lucy Carson, related to the frontiersman Kit Carson. Together, he and Lucy had ten children, all of whom had formal education due to Blackburn's tireless work ethic. Blackburn died in 1951 at the age of 108.

George Freeman Bragg was born as a slave in Warrenton, North Carolina, but he and his family very quickly became free after the Civil War. Religion had always been a huge part of Bragg's upbringing; he was baptized at Emmanuel Episcopal Church, and his family later moved to Petersberg, Virginia, to live with his grandmother Caroline Wiley Cain Bragg, a former slave of an Episcopal priest and a devout Episcopalian herself. Caroline became one of the founding members of Petersberg's first Black Episcopalian church, St. Steven's Episcopal Church. Bragg attended St. Stephen's parochial school until 1870 when he was expelled for a lack of humility. He founded the weekly

Black newspaper *The Lancet* (eventually known as *The Afro-American Churchman* and the *Church Advocate*) in 1882 and returned to parochial school in 1885. He was finally ordained as a deacon in 1887 and received his ordination as an Episcopal priest in 1888. Bragg died in 1940.

Dr. Anna Julia Haywood Cooper was born into slavery in 1858, but later became one of the nation's most prominent African American scholars. Known as "the mother of Black Feminism," she earned her PhD in history from the University of Paris-Sorbonne in 1924, making her the fourth Black woman to earn a doctoral degree.

Much of Cooper's focus was on the importance of keeping African American folklore alive. Because she realized the importance of cataloging the oral tales told by Black families, she cofounded the Washington Negro Folklore Society to collect and preserve these stories. Her book *A Voice from the South* (1892) is considered the first book about the African American experience from a feminist perspective and focuses on suffrage, poverty, segregation, Black literature, and more. She later became the second president of the Frelinghuysen University, which offered vocational, religious, and academic education for Black working class adults. Even though the school earned and lost its accreditation within the decade of 1927 to 1937, Cooper continued to make the school (renamed the Frelinghuysen Group of Schools for Colored Working People) an avenue for Black Americans to take when advancing their careers. She remained with the school until 1942. She, like Moore, lived to the old age of 105.

Going Forward After Slavery

Although those who were enslaved were stripped of their magnanimous titles and prestige and, indeed, their human rights, they managed to keep their dignity through sheer force of will. It is their survival instinct that is present in Black American history today, and that instinct helped propel many of the country's inventors, businesspeople, activists, artists, scientists, doctors, eco-warriors, and many more achieve their dreams and change American society in the process.

THE BOOK OF

Awesome

BLACK
AMERICANS

Chapter 2

Making Boss Moves

Much of Black America's history was affected by the country's human rights abuses. Clearly, America has not been particularly kind to the Black American. However, even with an entire country set against them, the Africans who were brought to the West as slaves still fought for a better life and many actually achieved it in many disciplines, including business. In the eighteenth and (part of) the nineteenth centuries, it would have been impossible for many to believe that Black men and women could own businesses, employ hundreds or even thousands, and invent some of the most important products America has ever seen.

As a person living in the twenty-first century, it is probably impossible for you to remember a time when there weren't Black movers and shakers in the world, building businesses, making lucrative deals, and reaching the monetary height of success. We should be thankful for that success, since it's anecdotal proof that, despite all of the setbacks, our country has made societal progress. Today's Black businesspeople can look like you and me, setting out into the world of entrepreneurship. Or they can look like bigwig rappers like **Jay-Z** and **P. Diddy**, two rappers who were able to transform their music careers into lucrative businesses.

Jay-Z is behind the music distribution company Tidal but has many other companies to his name, such as the urban fashion line Rocawear and the music publishing and artist management/touring company Roc Nation, and he's part owner of the New Jersey Nets, among other ventures. Diddy, on the other hand, made his most famous business mark with his clothing line Sean John. He has since made inroads in the wine and spirits category with his deals with Diageo's Ciroc and DeLeon tequila. He also co-owns AQUAhydrate water with Mark Wahlberg and has a stake of Revolt, a popular television network.

Today's Black entrepreneurs and businesspeople come from all walks of life, from the wealthy to the bootstrappers. It's great that we live in a time where we have so many examples of Black businessowners that we can be inspired to follow our dreams.

It wasn't always this way. Many years ago, all we might have heard about were White businesspeople and their achievements, and it would have been tough to find examples of strong Black businesses unless you knew where to look. But they were out there, and they were laying the groundwork for business-minded Black Americans like Jay-Z, P. Diddy, and others to follow behind.

Early Pioneers

Black Americans have been masters at making a way out of no way and creating a decent life for themselves despite everything that was stacked against them. Some, like **Benjamin Banneker**, went above and beyond and showcased savant-like talents that progressed a nation, even while that same nation was trying to keep him and those like him suppressed. Banneker was born

a free man in 1731 Virginia and, as such, he attended Quaker schools. Thanks to the Quaker anti-racist philosophy, he probably grew up in a blessed bubble of protection against the harsh, racist outside world. However, he left school after the second grade and was self-taught afterwards. He was apparently his best teacher, since he excelled in many areas, including engineering, astronomy, mathematics, writing and public speaking.

Banneker was easily one of the smartest people in the eighteenth century, replicating the blueprints for Washington, DC, from memory after the man hired for the job, Pierre Charles L'Enfant, left his position as engineer in a huff and took the plans with him. He also built the first clock in America, which worked perfectly for forty years. Another of his accomplishments includes his annual farmer's almanac, which he created after becoming interested in astronomy (and successfully predicting an eclipse from his own calculations). The almanac contains information all drawn from Banneker's mathematic and scientific know-how and became a top-selling book in several states including those in the original thirteen colonies as well as those closer to the South like Kentucky, a tremendous feat for the first book of science, and one of the first published works, written by an African American author.

Banneker's almanac was useful for farmers of all stripes, but one of the most important uses he had for it was as a weapon against racism and war. One of his tactics included sending a copy to Thomas Jefferson, who had hired him to replicate plans for the capital. Although Jefferson's most famous line from the Declaration of Independence was, "all men are created equal," he wasn't a practitioner of what he preached; he owned hundreds of slaves on his property, Monticello, and kept Sally Hemmings as what many would have called back then a "mistress," although in reality she was a victim of his sexual abuse, since slaves didn't have the right to consent. How can you change the mindset of a man whose own behavior is wildly hypocritical? It's not known if Banneker thought his plan of sending his almanac was a long shot, but he sent it anyway, with the goal to impress upon Jefferson that his own words of men being created equal should stand for Black men, too. However, despite Jefferson's words of praise, he failed to implement any action against slavery, which is why Jefferson consistently gets an L in history for being one of the country's biggest hypocrites, a man full of flowery words but no backbone to implement them in reality.

Regardless of being unable to change Jefferson, Banneker charged forward when it came to speaking out against injustice, whether that was through his inventions or his almanac, his work as a farmer, surveyor, engineer and city planner, or through his writings as an author or his research as a mathematician and astronomer. Banneker and others like him provided inspiration for those looking to make a better life for themselves, even with slavery and discrimination staring them in the face. That drive kept up even after the Civil War, when many Black Americans were excited to start life as free Americans.

After the Civil War, America was ready for Reconstruction, which took place from 1865 to 1877. This period was supposed to establish Black Americans as independent, self-sufficient citizens. Instead, Reconstruction was a volatile time in which freed Blacks faced violent racism, often resulting in lynchings, burnings, and other fearmongering tactics. It can be argued that Reconstruction was doomed from the beginning, since President Abraham Lincoln, the architect of Reconstruction, was assassinated one week after the end of the Civil War and the abolition of slavery. Even though Andrew Johnson, Lincoln's Vice President, assumed Lincoln's Reconstruction policies after he took over the presidential office, states as far up across the Mason-Dixon line as the Midwest began installing rules to limit Black economic and social progression.

It can also be argued that Reconstruction didn't last long enough to establish any kind of nationwide social sea change. Once the initiative became dismantled via Lincoln's assassination and Southern and Midwestern states undermining the government, the idealistic notion of Reconstruction became something like a pipe dream. However, Black Americans had survived slavery through sheer will and ingenuity—they didn't have the support of the government when they needed it during slavery, and they weren't going to limit themselves after slavery just because of this lack of support.

Despite states trying to limit progress, even with violent measures, Black Americans persisted throughout the trauma and established themselves as prominent business leaders, inventors and economic innovators.

Inventors and businesspeople like Banneker and others from the eighteenth century showcased the intelligence of the Black mind, one that was able to reach for the stars despite Black Americans being shackled on the ground, whether by actual shackles or the societal shackles placed on free Black people. That uplifting outlook on life can be found in the life of **Clara Brown**, who was a slave in Virginia before becoming a community leader and philanthropist. As a philanthropist, she helped former slaves acclimate to free life in Denver, Colorado, during the state's Gold Rush. Brown became the first Black woman to reside in Denver after arriving in 1859, and she's believed to be the first Black woman to take part in the Colorado

Gold Rush. Brown was also a business owner, opening a laundry shop wherever she went, including in Denver.

That entrepreneurial spirit can also be found in the area of Tulsa, Oklahoma, once known as **Black Wall Street.** Black Wall Street was the nickname for Greenwood Avenue in the suburb of Greenwood. Greenwood Avenue was a breath of fresh air in America since it was home to hundreds of prosperous Black-owned businesses. It became a hot zone for commerce because of Tulsa's oil boom in the early 1900s, which attracted many Black Americans from the South. It's ironic that Oklahoma's Jim Crow laws, which in the Southern and some Midwestern states prohibited Blacks from working, socializing, and living in general alongside Whites, helped Black Wall Street grow. Because Blacks couldn't do business in the same areas as White Oklahomans, the isolation forced Black businesses to innovate, starting with **O.W. Gurley**, the entrepreneur who established Black Wall Street in 1906.

Gurley was a wealthy Black landowner who had a presidential appointment from President Grover Cleveland before he moved from Arkansas to Oklahoma to take part in 1889's Oklahoma Land Run. When he came to Tulsa in 1906, he bought forty acres of land, which became Greenwood Avenue, named in honor of a city in Mississippi. Gurley also established Vernon AME Church, which was destroyed during the Tulsa race riots and rebuilt in 1928. More on that tragedy later.

All of the businesses were owned by Black businesspeople and catered exclusively to Black clientele. Despite Oklahoma's systematic racism, however, both White and Black Tulsans patronized the shops and businesses in Black Wall Street.

Black Wall Street exhibited the business power of Black Americans when given the chance. The area became home to many Black multimillionaires, and, if this area was a White-owned neighborhood, Tulsa wouldn't have had a problem. But because it was run exclusively by wealthy Black Tulsans, the White community felt threatened by their success. So, the Tulsa riots arose after a nineteen-year-old shoe shiner named Dick Rowland allegedly assaulted seventeen-year-old Sarah Page, a White elevator operator in a White-owned building. Rowland only used the elevator to get to the building's bathroom, and Page herself never pressed charges. But with an opportunity present, armed White men rampaged Tulsa, with armed Black men rising up to protect Rowland. Today, the burning of Black Wall Street is known as domestic terrorism, but, at the time, it was seen as keeping Blacks in their place, based on the imaginary fear created by stereotypes and assumptions.

After Black Wall Street

We can be thankful that Black Wall Street wasn't the only place where Black business excellence thrived. Throughout the country, Black inventors, businesspeople, and innovators charged forward and created unimaginable lives for themselves. One of those businesspeople include **Garrett Morgan**, who started out life as the son of former slaves in Kentucky but became one of America's wealthiest men in the 1920s. As a young man, Morgan quickly used his business talents to better himself. Once he moved to Cleveland, Ohio, in 1895, he spent twelve years as a sewing machine repairman, saving enough money to start his own repair business. His one business soon turned into several businesses, including a tailoring business, a newspaper company which published the *Cleveland Call*, and a company that made personal grooming products. By the time 1920 rolled around, Morgan's empire made him extremely wealthy, allowing him to pass on working opportunities to his many workers.

Several of Morgan's inventions have helped shape America into the place it is today, such as the "safety hood" or gas mask, which he invented in 1916 after seeing firefighters struggle with smoke on the job. The device helped save a group of trapped miners who were stuck in a shaft under Lake Erie. The incident instantly made his gas mask a success, and he received orders from mine owners and fire departments throughout the US and Europe.

What's sad is that, at first, his contribution to saving the lives of the trapped miners was written out of the official story in Southern newspapers simply because he was a Black man. Eventually, that glaring omission was addressed, but regardless of whether Southern states wanted to acknowledge a Black man's invention, Morgan's gas mask became a staple in the lives of American first responders and the military. The mask not only helped save lives of firefighters and miners, but a slightly revamped version of the mask was given to soldiers in World War I. Morgan also invented the zigzag stitching attachment for sewing machines, now a must-have for sewing enthusiasts to create stitching for fabrics such as stretch knits. He also created a device we see and use every day—the traffic light.

Morgan was inspired to invent traffic lights after he witnessed a crash between a car and a buggy. He saw an opportunity to create a product that could give motorists and other vehicles ease of mind when sharing the road. He received his patent in America in 1923 and later patented his invention in Canada and Britain. Eventually, the traffic light made Morgan even more money to add to his empire; he sold his patent to General Electric for forty thousand dollars. Without his invention, just think of how unsafe travel would be. Morgan died in 1963 as a wealthy businessman, a far cry from his meager beginnings on his parents' Kentucky farm.

Annie Turnbo Malone was the woman whose work in beauty and hair care inspired Madam C.J. Walker to launch her own hair care business. Malone was born in 1869 in Metropolis, Illinois, as the tenth of eleven children. When her parents died, she lived with an older sister and went to school, although she wasn't able to graduate due to illness. But as her hometown's name suggests, Malone was already born super. Even though she didn't finish school, her time in class fostered her love for chemistry, and it was this love that led her toward creating her first product—one that helped Black women straighten their hair without damaging it.

Malone kept creating more products until she had an entire line for potential customers, and to gain those customers, she moved to St. Louis and went door to door, giving women live demonstrations. She also debuted her products at the 1904 World's Fair, one of the best ways to gain tons of publicity for a new product or service at the time. This amount of publicity gave her enough wind in her sails to launch her company, Turnbo's Poro Company. She eventually married St. Louis school principal, Aaron E. Malone, and through her company's success became a millionaire by the end of World War I. She used her wealth in charitable ways to help Black American organizations and philanthropic groups and established the cosmetology school Poro College in St. Louis.

Malone's success in haircare paved the way for others, including **Madam C.J. Walker**. I feel we know more about Walker because of her ability to market herself as a brand alongside her business. She utilized her image as its own type of selling point, similar to how celebrities today use their status to sell products or business ventures or, for the Gen Z crowd, beauty YouTubers endear themselves to their audience by becoming an inviting personality. Her flair for the dramatic helped propel her to superstar status, but thankfully, she also used her fame to help other Black women find opportunity.

Born Sarah Breedlove, Walker was the daughter of slaves-turned-sharecroppers in Louisiana. Similar to Malone, Walker became an orphan during her childhood and lived with her older sister and worked in the cotton fields with her.

Her early life continued to be harrowing: she married at age fourteen as an escape from her sister's abusive husband. But her husband, Moses McWilliams, died, leaving Walker a single mother to her daughter Lelia, or, as she came to be known, A'Lelia. Her second marriage to John Davis was also troubled, and the two eventually divorced. Throughout that time, though, Walker did her best to provide for her daughter by moving near her four brothers in St. Louis and earned work as a cook and laundress.

Her brothers' profession, barbering, was a bit of foreshadowing as to what Walker's life would become. She became devoted to Anne Turbo Malone's "The Great Wonderful Hair Grower" product to recover from hair loss, presumably from stress. Her love for the product led her to become one of Malone's Black saleswomen and eventually, Walker launched her own hair line with just $1.25. By this time, she had moved to Denver, Colorado, and was married once again, this time to an ad man named Charles Joseph Walker, and renamed herself "Madam C.J. Walker" to launch her line.

This third marriage didn't last long either, but the name and her husband's business acumen helped Walker establish her line and grow her Walker Manufacturing Company in Indianapolis, Minnesota. Like Malone, she also hired a line of Black women for her sales team and eventually employed forty thousand Black men and women throughout the US, Canada, and the Caribbean. She became a millionaire, owned a mansion in Irvington, New York, as well as several properties in Harlem, St. Louis, Chicago, and Pittsburgh and established the Negro Cosmetics Manufacturers Association, helping Black businessowners network and coalesce as a powerful business force.

One of the Black women Walker inspired was **Marjorie Stewart Joyner**, who was one of Madam C.J. Walker's contemporaries and became a huge part of Walker's business as part of her board of directors. Joyner was born in Virginia in 1896, and her family moved to Chicago as part of the Great Migration north for jobs and opportunities. She met her future husband, Robert Joyner, who was studying podiatry. While he was in school, she went to the A.B. Molar Beauty School and became the school's first Black graduate. Afterwards, she opened her beauty salon, where she became known for her prowess at setting Marcel waves, a popular style at the time. It so happened that when she tried to set her mother-in-law's hair, she failed, which prompted her mother-in-law to pay for her to attend classes to learn how to work on Black people's hair. As it turns out, that class was taught by Walker, and she was so impressed with Joyner that she offered her a job. Even though Joyner turned her down because of her new marriage, the two stayed in contact and, eventually, Joyner became one of Walker's demonstrators who traveled throughout the nation teaching others Walker's famous hair tips.

Joyner's own history with the Marcel wave led her to create a new invention—the waving machine, which can set an entire head of hair at the same time. She applied for her patent in 1928 and the machine took off. She never made a dime from her invention, since the patents belonged to Walker's company where Joyner was still an employee, but her career in hair launched her higher up the ladder: she eventually became the vice president of one of Walker's salon divisions and joined the board of directors. Joyner's presence in American society is even more cemented in her philanthropy work, including cofounding Florida's Bethune-Cookman College with Mary McLeod Bethune. It was at the college that she earned a BS in psychology in 1973. Joyner died at 1994 at the age of ninety-eight, but the spirit of her invention lives on in today's contemporary wavers. Today's wavers are handheld instead of looking like the intimidating apparatus Joyner invented, which was basically a hair dryer connected to several curling rods. Several handheld devices on the market today have the same multi-rod design embedded within their DNA, meaning that Joyner's unique invention has lasting merit.

Maggie L. Walker became the first Black woman in America to found a bank, a feat that is impressive to this day, since **Kiko Davis** is currently the only Black woman today who owns a bank. Born in Virginia after the Civil War, Maggie began her life of service to the community by joining the Independent Order of St. Luke, which helped the infirm and elderly and promoted humanitarian causes. She served as the Order's Right Worthy Grand Secretary from 1899 until her death in 1934.

Her banking career began in 1902 when she established the newspaper *The St. Luke Herald*, which helped the Order communicate with the public, and the St. Luke Penny Savings Bank in 1903 to help the people utilize their own money to help themselves. She served as the bank's president from the outset and later became chairwoman of the board when the bank merged with two other banks to become The Consolidated Bank and Trust Company. The bank was the oldest continually Black-operated bank in America until 2009.

It's unfortunate that Walker's achievement stands as a rarity in America today; Davis, currently the only woman who holds the same title Walker held decades ago, is the current owner of the tenth largest African American owned bank in the nation, First Independence Bank. Her ownership comes through being the trustee of the Donald Davis Living Trust, the majority stockholder of the bank. Even though the statistic of Black women in bank ownership remains unfortunately low, Davis and Walker show that it is possible for women to achieve anything they set their minds to.

Bridget "Biddy" Mason was born as a slave in Mississippi in 1818, but little did anyone know that she would grow up to become one of the first prominent citizens and landowners in Los Angeles. Throughout her turbulent early life, which included being uprooted several times to live in Georgia and South Carolina with other slaveowners before being returned to Mississippi to become the slave of Robert Marion Smith. As a Mormon, Smith moved his family and slaves to establish a Mormon community in what was then Mexican territory. That community would become Salt Lake City, Utah.

Mason's turbulent life also included meeting free Black couple Charles H. and Elizabeth Flake, who told her to legally fight her slave status once she and her slaveowner reached California, where Smith wanted to move to despite California's laws against slavery. After spending five years in California as a slave, she did legally challenge Smith for her freedom, which she earned via the court. She eventually became a midwife and a nurse and used her earnings to buy land in what is now downtown Los Angeles. She also established Los Angeles's First AME Church, the city's oldest Black church. Her wealth, which she used for charitable endeavors and for establishing an elementary school for Black children and a traveler's aid center, was estimated at three million dollars. Mason died in 1891.

Mary Ellen Pleasant was an abolitionist who helped slaves escape with the Underground Railroad, helped finance John Brown's failed slave uprising, and sued San Francisco for Black Americans' right to use streetcars. Pleasant spent her childhood in Philadelphia and worked with the Hussey family in their store. After her service to the Hussey family ended in her twenties, she became a tailor's assistant and a church organist. It was during that time that she met her first husband, James. W. Smith, a rich plantation owner with African ancestry from his Cuban heritage. Smith had gone through his own journey before he met Pleasant; by the time they finally met, he had pledged himself to the abolitionist movement.

Interestingly enough, both Pleasant and Smith were able to pass for White people, which they used to their advantage. However, Pleasant knew very well how her bread was buttered. She might have utilized her privilege to advance in the corporate world, but she used her earnings to advance the cause of civil rights. For instance, during her first marriage, she became friends with abolitionists William Lloyd Garrison and Wendell Phillips, the latter of whom promised her his estate if she kept fighting for the end of slavery. Pleasant and Smith also were a part of the Underground Railroad, helping slaves escape to Canada.

Pleasant eventually remarried, this time to JJ Pleasant, a shipboard cook who decided to try his luck in the California Gold Rush. Pleasant followed him with the hopes of running a boarding house and restaurant. Her restaurant, which became known as "Black City Hall," was where Black Americans who arrived in San Francisco after slavery could find work. She later invested in a boarding house for wealthy businessmen in the area as well as a Sonoma Valley ranch that included a vineyard and horse-racing track.

When most people think of the lightbulb, they think of Thomas Edison, but the story of the lightbulb continues with **Lewis Latimer**, the son of runaway slaves who grew up to work at a patent law firm after his stint in the Navy during the Civil War. It was during his time with inventor Hiram Maxim at the US Electric Lighting Company that he patented the carbon filament for the incandescent lightbulb. This small invention made lightbulbs more affordable and accessible for families, which made electricity more accessible for all. Latimer later worked with Thomas Edison in 1890 at the Edison Electric Light Company as a patent expert and chief draftsman. While at Edison, he wrote the book *Incandescent Electric Lighting: A Practical Description of the Edison System*. Latimer's electrical expertise led him to become one of the company's charter members. Electricity wasn't all Latimer was interested in. He also put his mind toward the telephone. While the credit is given to Alexander Graham Bell, it is actually Latimer's drawings that Bell used to patent the telephone in 1876.

These early businessmen and women have provided the groundwork for future Black businesspeople to follow in their footsteps.

Businesspeople of the Twentieth Century

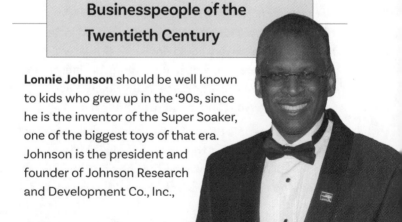

Lonnie Johnson should be well known to kids who grew up in the '90s, since he is the inventor of the Super Soaker, one of the biggest toys of that era. Johnson is the president and founder of Johnson Research and Development Co., Inc., as well as several other companies in science and real estate. As a Tuskegee graduate, he started out his career as a research engineer at Oak Ridge National Laboratory before joining the Air Force and serving as the acting chief of the Air Force Weapons Laboratory's Space Nuclear Power Safety Section. In 1979, he joined NASA as a Senior Systems Engineer within their Jet Propulsion Laboratory, where he was part of the team that worked on the Galileo mission to Jupiter. He returned to the Air Force in 1982 and acted as the Advanced Space Systems Requirements Officer at Strategic Air Command. He also came back to NASA's Jet Propulsion Laboratory in 1987, where he worked on the Mars Observer project and was the fault protection engineer during the beginning stages of NASA's Cassini project.

After his time in NASA, he created his own engineering firm in 1989 and developed the toy that became every kid's dream, the Super Soaker. He licensed his invention to the Larami Corporation, and the toy was an instant hit, earning over two hundred million dollars in sales and becoming the number one toy in the nation. The toy became even bigger once Larami was sold to Hasbro, the second largest toy manufacturer in the US. The Super Soaker isn't Johnson's only invention; he has over a hundred patents to his name with over twenty more pending, and his products include a new generation of rechargeable battery technology and thermodynamic energy conversion technology.

James Edward Maceo West has helped many in the music business create better sounding art. Born in Virginia in 1931, West currently holds over 250 US and foreign patents for microphone design and production and techniques for creating polymer foil electrets. West received a master's degree in physics from Temple University in 1957. In 1962, West invented the foil electret microphone while working on instruments for human hearing research. The invention has had immense popularity throughout the industry; about 90 percent of more than two billion microphones are based on this invention. Even more impressive: many of our everyday products, including camcorders, telephones, baby monitors, recording devices and hearing aids are also built with this invention. West continues changing the world with his inventions. His latest one? A device to detect pneumonia in the lungs of infants. And for Black American burgeoning inventors, West provides support with the Corporate Research Fellowship Program for graduate students pursuing terminal degrees in the sciences. Combined with his Summer Research Program, he has given five hundred non-White grad students their chance in the science industry. West also cofounded the Association of Black Laboratory Employees. The group was formed to address the concerns of Black employees within Bell Laboratories.

You know that home security system many parents have? The one that kids have to remember the code for? Guess what? It's a high-tech version of the original system developed by a Black woman who wanted to feel safer in her neighborhood. **Marie Van Brittan Brown** is credited with inventing the home security system. Born in 1922 in New York City, Brown, who worked as a nurse by trade, came up with her idea for the closed-circuit television security system in 1966 with her husband Albert Brown when she realized the police in her area were responding too slowly to emergencies on her street. She probably felt like she'd have to rely on herself since the actual police weren't doing their job. Thus, the home security system was born, so Brown could have peace of mind while staying at home alone.

One could see her invention as an indictment on the local police, since it's not said whether or not the police were slow to her neighborhood because of racist reasons or because of an actual backlog of crime they were trying to attend to. We can give them the benefit of the doubt and say that maybe the police were understaffed. Regardless, Brown's invention showed that there was a gap in the city's protection services for its citizens, and her invention found a needy market that still exists today.

Her system is essentially what all home security systems are based on; even though there have been some twenty-first century updates including smartphone technology, the basic setup for home security rests on Brown's original idea. Brown was given the Award for the National Scientists Committee for her invention. She died in 1999.

Heart health is what many Americans are concerned with today, and one of the ways Americans find relief is through the installation of a pacemaker, which helps regulate the heart's beating functions. Many Americans have to give thanks to **Otis Boykin** who created the pacemaker, which has saved countless lives.

Born in Texas in 1920, Boykin graduated from Fisk College in 1941 and started his career at Magic Radio and TV Corporation and Nilsen Research Laboratories. Boykin invented products on his own while he tried to develop his own company, Boykin-Fruth Incorporated, with twenty-six patents associated with him, including the control unit for the pacemaker as well as the wire precision resistor used in TVs and radios. He also created a device that can withstand extreme temperature changes and pressure. Because it was cheaper and more reliable than others like it already out there, Boykin's device became highly sought after by IBM for computers and the US military for guided missiles. It's darkly ironic that he died in 1982 from heart failure of all things. Boykin's inventions have helped doctors and surgeons give many Americans a new lease on life. So if your parents or grandparents are able to have renewed health because of a pacemaker, pour some out for Boykin, who made it all possible.

Frederick McKinley Jones's inventions have impacted many areas of American life, from refrigeration to movie theaters. Born in 1893 in Ohio, he served in World War I in France before coming home and starting a job as a garage mechanic. Jones began inventing based on his own self-taught knowledge, with his first invention being a self-starting gasoline motor. As he transitioned from mechanic work toward working at a steamship and a hotel, he did more inventing and design work, including designing and building racecars after moving to Hallock, Minnesota. Incredibly, one of his cars, Number 15, was able to drive faster than an airplane.

Jones's jack of all trades mentality kept him inventing new products, including adapters for silent movie projectors, allowing movie theaters to play talking films. He also invented a machine for the box office that issued tickets and provided change to customers. For those of you who have grown up in snowy areas, you might be accustomed to seeing a snowmobile or two—Jones invented that too.

The area he has the most patents in, however, is in refrigeration with forty total. One of those inventions includes the first automatic refrigeration system for long-haul trucks and railroad cars, which eliminated food spoilage during shipping and allowed Americans all across the country to eat fresh produce no matter where they lived. His work in refrigeration led him to create the Thermo-King Corporation in 1935, where he continued to change the world of long-distance food shipping. Jones died in 1961.

Atlanta owes a debt of thanks to **Herman J. Russell**, who started his real estate empire in 1946 by buying a lot where he would build a duplex. This property started Russell's business of creating business in segregated Atlanta by developing many real estate investments and creating a construction company that would become one of the largest Black-owned companies in the nation and the largest Minority Business Enterprise (MBE) real estate firm in the country.

Russell's slate of businesses includes H.J. Russell and Company, the umbrella company which housed other companies including H.J. Russell Construction Company, Paradise Management Inc., DDR International, H. J. Russell Plastering Company and Southeast Land Development Company. Russell's projects turned Atlanta into what it is today, with buildings such as the Hartsfield-Jackson Atlanta International Airport, Philips Arena (now known as State Farm Arena), Turner Field and the Georgia Dome—all included in his portfolio. By 1994, H. J. Russel and Company grossed around $150 million with offices throughout the country, including in Miami and New York City.

Russell also used his money to help further Black prosperity by becoming the first Black member and eventually the second Black president of the Atlanta Chamber of Commerce. He contributed to the success of Maynard Jackson's mayoral election campaign, leading to Jackson becoming Atlanta's first Black mayor, and he also helped behind the scenes with the civil rights movement with friends like Martin Luther King Jr.

Reginald Lewis is described as the "richest Black man in America," and was estimated to be worth at least one billion dollars by 1992. Lewis's status made his business, TLC Beatrice International, the first Black-owned business to gross one billion d0llars in annual sales. Born in 1942 in Baltimore, Lewis attended Harvard Law School as the only person in the history of the school to be admitted before actually applying. In 1970, he and his associates established the first

Black-owned law firm in Wall Street and used his legal expertise to develop investments in minority-owned businesses, which led him to become special counsel for big brands such as Equitable Life (now known as AXA) and General Foods. He also worked as counsel for the Commission for Racial Justice and successfully lobbied for North Carolina to pay interest on the bond for the Wilmington Ten, nine men and one woman who were wrongly convicted of arson and conspiracy in 1971 and served almost ten years in jail before an appeal granted them release.

The road to one billion d0llars started with Lewis's TLC Group, L.P., established in 1983. The first acquisition he made under his new company was the McCall Pattern Company, which he bought for $22.5 million. Under his leadership, McCall's had two of its most profitable years in its 113-year history, and in 1987, he sold McCalls for $65 million. He was also able to buy Beatrice Foods for $985 million, making his company the only US company to engage in the largest leverage buyout of overseas assets at the time. The newly restructured company, TLC Beatrice International, became the one billion dollar juggernaut that made Lewis a history-making Black businessman. Unfortunately, Lewis died unexpectedly in 1993 at the age of fifty due to a short illness. His legacy has certainly paved the way for others like rapper-turned Tidal mogul Jay-Z, who famously rapped, "I'm not a businessman, I'm a business, *man*."

Blackness in Business

What can we learn from these men and women? I think the best thing we can take away is how much Black history surrounds us, even when we aren't thinking about it. When you look at a traffic light or a simple zigzag stitch on a piece of clothing, you're looking at a Black American invention. When you buy hair products or set your alarm system, you're looking at the impact of Black Americans on our everyday lives. There is no part of America that Black Americans haven't impacted, and it shows how we are a much more integral part of society than the history books would lead you to think.

Little-Known Civil Rights Leaders

So far in this book, we have been traveling through earlier periods of American history. Even though the "civil rights movement" as we understand it isn't linked to times like the 1700s, 1800s, and even the early 1900s, the movement's core beliefs were alive in abolitionist and likeminded groups. However, the civil rights movement as we know it began in the 1940s and grew to its zenith in the 1960s.

Conventional wisdom would tell us that the movement ended in the late '60s and early '70s with the murders of several civil rights leaders such as Martin Luther King Jr., Malcolm X, Medgar Evers, and several others, including regular, everyday citizens like Emmett Till who were killed for simply being Black. But that's where conventional wisdom is wrong. The civil rights movement continues today with social media-turned-real world groups such as Black Lives Matter, Dream Defenders, and others.

But before we get into the present and future, we must understand the foremothers and forefathers who laid the groundwork. We must give thanks to those who put their lives on the line to create better opportunities for us today.

Unsung Heroes

We know the usual names: Martin Luther King, Rosa Parks, Malcolm X, Congressman John Lewis. You have to wonder what the rest of the movement was like beyond these usual suspects. What are the stories we either haven't heard or know very little about?

For me, the beauty of the civil rights movement is that it included everyone who wanted to participate. You didn't have to be a pastor with a large congregation or the leader of an activist group. You could have been a regular person whose only claim to fame was taking care of your family. But if you contributed to the betterment of your family and others by marching for the right to vote, boycotting businesses, or attending a local NAACP chapter meeting, you could have considered yourself a civil rights activist.

With that said, it's interesting how much politics and optics were a consideration in the movement. You might have already learned about the positive ways in which movement leaders utilized the media to propel their message, which involved putting their own lives on the line for newspapers to cover the injustices happening in the South. But there were also some negatives when utilizing the media, which came in the form of figuring out *who* could be the face of certain events and who couldn't. Even though the fight was to change social mores, leaders oftentimes had to work within those same social mores to get anything done. Case in point with a young girl named **Claudette Colvin**, who actually refused to give up her bus seat in

Montgomery, Alabama, nine months before Rosa Parks did in 1955.

Colvin told the White bus driver who wanted her to give up her bus seat to a White passenger, "It's my constitutional right to sit here as much as that lady. I paid my fare, it's my constitutional right." She was arrested for violating Alabama's segregation laws, even though she was clearly correct—it *was* her constitutional right to sit wherever she wanted.

So why did the civil rights rally happen around Parks instead of Colvin? Turns out the NAACP felt her case wasn't the right one to litigate. Colvin was a pregnant teenager at the time she decided to challenge the segregation laws, and the association felt that Colvin being an unwed, single, teenage mother would be a distraction from the actual problem of discrimination at hand. Still, Colvin brought her case to court and declared herself not guilty. Unfortunately, her reputation was run through the gutter because of her pregnancy, and she was forced to drop out of college; the lies about her reputation also made it hard for her to find work. Eventually, though, Colvin was one of the four plaintiffs in the *Browder v. Gayle* case in which Montgomery's segregated buses were ruled unconstitutional. After the case, she moved to New York City and, now a mother of two children, she became a nurse's aide in a nursing home until she retired in 2004.

Parks, on the other hand, became the face of the bus boycott nine months after Colvin's decision to stay in her seat. Of course, this isn't meant to shade Parks; she is a valuable part of the movement. However, it is important to recognize how fighting for civil rights is as much of a political game as it was a social rights fight. While Colvin was a teenage mother, Parks was a seamstress in Montgomery. Her arrest led **E.D. Nixon**, the head of the Montgomery chapter of the NAACP, to begin creating a structured plan to fight back against the bus system. As we now know, the bus boycott was a success. But that ball got rolling because of unsung heroes like Colvin who threw the first stone at Montgomery's discriminatory laws.

Another unsung hero in the civil rights movement is **Bayard Rustin.** It's only been in recent years that Rustin's importance to Martin Luther King Jr. has been explored. Sadly, it could be argued that the main reason historians have discounted his achievements in the civil rights movement is because he was a gay man.

Thankfully, King didn't care about Rustin's orientation and considered him one of his closest friends. Indeed, Rustin can be considered the architect behind King's nonviolence philosophy since Rustin was the one who introduced King to Mahatma Gandhi's nonviolent resistance techniques. Gandhi's philosophy was a part of Rustin's own activism before meeting King in 1955. Rustin combined Gandhi's work with African American labor leader—and Rustin's mentor and friend—**A. Philip Randolph**'s socialism theory, as well as his own Quaker pacifist background. Some of Rustin's activist work before his work with King includes joining forces with the American Friends Service Committee in 1941 to protect Japanese Americans' property during their unjust internment. He and a group of activists also took a trip throughout the South after World War II. Since he had been a conscientious objector to the war, he had already been arrested in 1944. This road trip meant he'd be arrested yet again, but this experience would come in handy much later.

Some of the key moments within the civil rights movement were organized in part by Rustin, including King's Montgomery bus boycott in 1956. Yes, the same bus boycott that involved Claudette Colvin (whose civil rights stance was written off because she was cast as a jezebel teen mom) and Rosa Parks. In fact, it was Rudolph himself that told Rustin to meet with King, which led to their friendship. The Freedom Rides that occurred throughout the South were also inspired by Rustin's own fateful ride, and so was the infamous March on Washington for Jobs and Freedom in 1963, during which King gave his "I Have A Dream" speech. Two years later, he went further back to his labor activist roots by cofounding the A. Philip Randolph Institute for Black trade union members.

This is a lot of work for one man to take part in, but somehow in between all of this, Rustin still had time to organize a march overseas. In 1958, Rustin was one of the coordinators of an anti-nuclear weapons march in Aldermaston, England. Clearly, as we saw by the huge turnout at the March on Washington five years later, Rustin had a knack for bringing out the masses. At the Aldermaston march, ten thousand people showed up to stand against nuclear weapons.

King and Rustin were considered close confidantes, and some people within King's circle wanted the civil rights leader to distance himself from Rustin; they feared that enemies to the movement would use their closeness against them, for political gain. This tension came to a head when King, Rustin, and Randolph were planning a march during the 1960 Democratic Convention of then-presidential candidate John F. Kennedy and vice-presidential candidate Lyndon B. Johnson. The protest was meant to call attention to the Democrats' lack of action on civil rights. But the party probably found this an opportune moment to keep King (and in the process, Rustin) silent by delegating a Black congressman, Adam Clayton Powell, to threaten the group with a lie. Powell, who didn't even face the group himself, sent a messenger to tell King, Rustin, and Rudolph that if they went through with the march, Powell would accuse King of having a sexual affair with Rustin, which could bring the civil rights movement to a screeching halt. After having counsel with his inner circle, including his confidant, speech writer, and advisor **Clarence Jones**, King did a rare thing—he conceded to pressure and began to distance himself from Rustin who then resigned from his post at the Southern Christian Leadership Conference.

After King's assassination in 1968, Rustin kept up the fight against inequality throughout the 1970s, including through his books *Down the Line* and *Strategies for Freedom*. As a man who was openly gay all of his life (even when it got him arrested in the fifties), he also advocated for LGBT rights in his activist work.

Rustin isn't the only civil rights activist whose work and very existence intersect race with sexual identity. Within the same timespan in 1969, the Stonewall Uprising occurred. You probably know the story—the Stonewall Inn served as ground zero for the beginning of the modern gay liberation movement. But the story wouldn't have been told without **Miss Major** and **Marsha P. Johnson**, two of the three trans women who led the uprising. Miss Major and Johnson were already activists before the Stonewall Uprising, and they continued fighting the good fight afterwards.

Miss Major, for instance, became part of the Trans Gender Variant and Intersex Justice Project, which she eventually led as executive director until her retirement in 2015. Johnson continued working with the other trans activist who led the Stonewall Uprising, Sylvia Rivera, to cofound the Street Transgender Action Revolutionaries. Sadly, her life was tragically taken and her body found in the Hudson River. It's still unclear how she died; her death was ruled a suicide, but those in her circle beg to differ. Thankfully, her case was reopened in 2017 by crime victim advocate Victoria Cruz.

Along with Rustin, King had other mentors who surrounded him, including **Ralph D. Abernathy**, whom King called "the best friend that I have in the world." A pastor by trade like King—the two met after becoming pastors at nearby churches in Montgomery, Alabama—

Abernathy helped King organize the Montgomery bus boycotts and cofounded the Southern Christian Leadership Conference.

The church was a part of Abernathy's life ever since he was a child; his father William was a farmer on their five hundred acres of land as well as a deacon in their local church. Abernathy was drafted into service during World War II, but, thankfully, he was able to survive and came back home to pursue a life as a minister while earning his mathematics degree from Alabama State College, which he received in 1950. He also earned his sociology degree from Atlanta University in 1951 and became the pastor of Montgomery's First Baptist Church as well as Alabama State's dean of students.

Abernathy's civil rights work with King constantly put him in danger. For instance, during the 1956 bus boycott, Abernathy's church and home were hit by bombs. Throughout his and King's work with the Freedom Riders and the SCLC and during protests in Atlanta, Abernathy was arrested seventeen times. Abernathy was even present the fateful morning King was assassinated at the Lorraine Motel in Memphis, Tennessee. Abernathy can be thought of as a successor of sorts to King's legacy, since he took over the SCLC after King's martyrdom and organized 1968's Poor People's Campaign, which led to the creation of the Federal Food Stamps Program.

He published his autobiography *And the Walls Came Tumbling Down* in 1989, before his death in 1990.

Another of King's friends in the struggle was **Fred Shuttlesworth**. Like King and Abernathy, Shuttlesworth was a pastor, but I'd argue that he's known more for his activist work than preaching from the pulpit, even in Birmingham where he lived and worked.

As a Birminghamian, Shuttlesworth was a part of my life throughout my childhood and up until his death in 2011 for his consistent activism within the community. He was seen as one of the keepers of Birmingham's oral history of segregation, civil rights, and the fights that ensued for justice. Even after his death, his presence is still heavily felt in the city. The Birmingham International Airport, for example, has been renamed in his honor. He may have never become Birmingham's mayor, but Abernathy certainly ran—and still runs—the city with his legacy, a legacy that literally changed the city forever.

Shuttlesworth and Abernathy's careers had several parallels. As I mentioned, Shuttlesworth was a pastor like his civil rights compatriots. Like Abernathy, he also graduated from Alabama State College (known today as Alabama State University). He also earned his BA in ministerial institution at Selma University. Along with Abernathy, Rustin, and King, he cofounded the SCLC while serving as the pastor of Bethel Baptist Church in Birmingham. Throughout the city, he fought for civil rights including the hiring of more Black police officers and the establishment of the Alabama Christian Movement for Human Rights.

Also, like Abernathy, Shuttlesworth wasn't a stranger to threats on his life. His home was bombed on Christmas Day 1956. He and his wife were attacked by the Ku Klux Klan as they took their daughter to integrate her school. Throughout his career, he was arrested countless times.

Shuttlesworth did relocate to Cincinnati in the sixties, only moving back to Birmingham in 2007, but kept his activism in the South alive with his work with King as well as by providing safe lodging for the Freedom Riders in 1961. His love for his hometown actually drove him to convince King to use Birmingham as a ground zero of sorts for the civil rights movement and utilized marches, particularly ones involving the socially activated young people of the city, to achieve change. He also took his fight even further south to Selma, where he organized the 1965 march from Selma to Montgomery for voting rights.

Abernathy and Shuttlesworth are both Alabamians, but, as a Birminghamian, I have to say that I'm immensely proud of Shuttlesworth's impact on my hometown, an impact I can still feel today because without his activism, Birmingham might not be the forward-looking beacon of hope in Alabama that is today.

Women of the Movement

While we hear a lot about the men of the movement, the women often become something of an afterthought. We know of **Coretta Scott King**, sure. But do we know that she was an activist in her own right and kept the fight for civil rights for all people alive after her husband's death? Do we know that she, along with recording artist Stevie Wonder, helped establish

Martin Luther King Jr. Day in 1986? I feel like that's a tidbit that gets routinely left out of the retelling of Coretta's life. She was a devoted mother and wife, accolades no one should take away from her. But she was also much more than the Black "June Cleaver" stereotype people paint her as. She was a woman who endured just as much pain as her husband from the frequent attacks on her husband and their family. She was a woman of character and dignity despite emotional turmoil from all sides. She managed to do it all with grace and courage until her death in 2006.

Her story has been routinely whitewashed by history, similar to how other women of the civil rights movement have either been neglected or whose contributions have been downplayed. Let's shine a light on them now.

Did you know King was friends with others in the civil rights movement, such as **Betty Shabazz?** Shabazz was the wife of **Malcolm X**.

Shabazz and King's friendship seems to me like one of the hidden gems of the civil rights movement. It wasn't until Lifetime's 2013 film *Betty & Coretta*, starring Mary J. Blige as Shabazz and Angela Bassett as Coretta, that I knew they ever spoke together, much less were close friends. However, it makes sense that they would be close; they both shared the burdens of being wives to the movement's most powerful leaders as well as mothers to families who were constantly put at risk.

In fact, Shabazz herself shielded her children with her body during the assassination of her husband.

After her husband's assassination in 1965, Shabazz had to call upon her strength to raise her children alone. The Nation of Islam, of which she and her husband were a part, reclaimed everything from her family. (A 1997 *Chicago Tribune* obituary says: "Everything the couple owned belonged to the Nation of Islam.") So she had to start over. Thanks to her supporters and friends, Shabazz was able to pick up the pieces of her life, earning a master's degree in public health from Jersey City State College and a PhD in education from the University of Massachusetts at Amherst and becoming a professor at Brooklyn's Medgar Evers College. Eventually, she became the director of the college's department of communications and public relations. Throughout her personal career, she also lectured about civil equality, keeping the torch of the civil rights movement alive.

Sadly, she was severely burned in 1997 after her twelve-year-old grandson set their New York apartment on fire. Her injuries resulted in her death. King did come to Shabazz's hospital bedside, according to minister and author Barbara Reynolds. "I know Shabazz's death was heartbreaking for King because she loved her," she wrote. "One a Muslim, the other a Christian; nevertheless, they were truly spiritual sisters. That is one truth I am certain of." Indeed, King is quoted as having called Shabazz a "wonderful caring person" who "carried forward her husband's legacy with dignity and grace." **Myrlie Evers-Williams**, a mutual friend of the two women and the widow of

Medgar Evers, who we'll learn about below, also spoke highly of Shabazz. Evers-Williams, an activist in her own right, said that she "has not been given the amount of credit she deserves in shaping America's civil rights movement."

One of the biggest names to come out of the youth activist group SNCC (Student Nonviolent Coordinating Committee) is Congressman John Lewis, who acted as the group's chairman. But **Diane Nash**, a lesser-known figure, finally made popular in Ava DuVernay's 2012 film *Selma*, is historic in her own right as well. As one of the founding members of the SNCC, she supported various initiatives to push for change, including providing support for the "Rock Hill Nine," nine students who were arrested and jailed for participating in a lunch counter sit-in in Rock Hill, South Carolina. She and fellow leaders **Charles Sherrod**, **Ruby Doris Smith**, and **Charles Jones** also staged a sit-in and refused bail, similar to the actions of the Rock Hill Nine. Nash also pushed for the Freedom Rides to continue even though the first Freedom Ride ended after being met with violence in Alabama. She told Shuttlesworth in 1961 that they were coming to Birmingham to continue the rides. Not only did they come to continue the rides, Nash herself led everyone from Birmingham to Jackson, Mississippi, in 1961.

Mary McLeod Bethune was a civil right activist from the generation before the one that took over in the 1950s and 1960s. However, her work is what future civil rights leaders drew from, intentionally or unintentionally.

Bethune was the daughter of former slaves, and, while her parents probably expected her to be better off than they were—Bethune took advantage of educational opportunities for African Americans after the Civil War—they probably never expected she'd run her own college.

She started her school, the Daytona Beach Literary and Industrial School for Training Negro Girls, after her marriage ended in 1904 and she was left trying to figure out how to take care of her son on her own. The school flourished and, after merging with Cookman Institute, an all-male school in Daytona, the result was Bethune-Cookman College, which is still in existence today.

Bethune was also a businesswoman as well as a civil rights activist—she owned a resort in Daytona and cofounded the Central Life Insurance Company of Tampa. But her activism is what made her known nationwide. Her work included leading many African Americans to migrate from the Republican Party to the Democratic Party during the Great Depression and acting as the director of Negro Affairs of the National Youth Administration under President Franklin

Roosevelt between 1936 and 1944. The position gave her the distinction of being the highest-ranking Black woman in American government, and her power lent itself to her efforts to end lynching and discrimination in America. Her longest position in politics was with the NAACP, which she ran as vice president until her death in 1955.

Bethune's activism inspired others like **Dorothy Height**, who joined the group Bethune founded and was president of the National Council of Negro Women. Within the group, Height also focused on ending lynching in America as well as leading efforts to revamp the criminal justice system which often worked against African Americans just as much back then as it does now.

It could be said that Height carried Bethune's proverbial baton forward in the race against injustice, since Height became the fourth president of the council and remained in the position for forty years. Under her leadership, the council gave financial aid to civil rights activists and supported voter registration in the Southern states. Like her predecessor, Height also became friends with Eleanor Roosevelt. She served as an advisor to Eleanor as well as presidents Dwight D. Eisenhower and Lyndon B. Johnson.

She also had a hand in organizing the March on Washington for Jobs and Freedom. But despite her work to get the march off the ground, as well as having a seat at the front of the march, she was not scheduled to speak. In fact, no women were scheduled to speak. This was indicative of the sexism that plagued the internal workings of the civil rights movement, a movement that had mostly men in its leadership. What else could explain the way Colvin was treated for being a teenage mother, or how Evers-Williams, Coretta, and Shabazz were treated as wives and widows? In the case of those three women, they were always reduced down to a second-tier position even though they were activists in their own right.

However, this didn't stop Height from her activist work, which eventually led her across the globe to India, where she served as a visiting professor at the University of Delhi, and South Africa, where she worked with the Black Women's Federation of South Africa. She earned numerous honorary degrees and awards during her lifetime, such as the Citizens Medal Award, the Congressional Gold Medal, and an induction into the Democracy Hall of Fame International. Hopefully at the time of her death in 2010 at the age of ninety-eight, she considered her life's work a job well done.

Amelia Boynton and her husband **Samuel William "S.W." Boynton** were activists in Selma, Alabama, years before the civil rights movement reached Alabama state lines. In fact, Boynton's childhood in Georgia was centered around leadership, with her mother being a suffragist and her father owning his own business, a wholesale wood lot. But her activism in Selma began around the time she met her husband in 1929. They were both working as agricultural extension agents in Selma and, together, they used their positions within the government to convince Black Americans to buy land and register to vote. They also owned several businesses, such as a real estate office, an employment agency and an insurance agency. In the mid-1930s, the Boyntons took over the Dallas County Voters League and welcomed SNCC when the group's leader Bernard Lafayette and his wife Colia Liddell came to town in 1962. Amelia Boynton also became the first Black woman in Alabama to run for Congress. Even though she didn't win, her campaign laid the groundwork for others to come behind her years later.

Boynton was one of the marchers during the first Selma to Montgomery march in 1965 that became known as "Bloody Sunday." In fact, she was one of the injured, enduring tear gas and beatings that rendered her unconscious. But she survived and remained an integral part of the voting rights movement. It was through her leadership, and the leadership of other activists, that Black Americans are allowed to vote.

Fannie Lou Hamer was also a civil rights activist who endured a different kind of injustice—forced sterilization. A White doctor sterilized Hamer without her consent during a surgery to remove a uterine tumor. This kind of forced sterilization was common and used as a way to "control" or limit the Black population, as if Black Americans were pests or weeds that were simply a nuisance instead of human beings with inalienable rights. In fact, the practice was so entrenched in Mississippi society, it became known as the "Mississippi appendectomy."

She became a SNCC organizer in 1962 after becoming enraged by the South's tricks to keep Black Americans from voting. Her efforts to demand voting rights included leading a group of seventeen to attempt to register to vote before being harassed and given a ridiculous literacy test. Even the school bus they rode on was fined for being "too yellow." Her action hit her family hard—she was fired from the plantation she and her husband worked on and her former employer confiscated most of their property.

But, in 1963, Hamer did successfully register to vote, leading her to protest other injustices, such as challenging the "Whites-only" segregated seating at a Charleston, South Carolina, bus station restaurant. She and other Black women in her party were beaten, and Hamer was left with injuries she would keep for the rest of her life, including kidney and leg damage as well as a blood clot in her eye.

However, none of that kept her down. She cofounded the Mississippi Freedom Democratic Party in 1964, challenging the Democratic Party's attempts to stuff down Black American participation. A speech she gave at the Democratic National Convention arguing for her group to be recognized as the official delegation was initially blocked from airtime by President Lyndon B. Johnson, who held a petty televised press conference just so she wouldn't get any airtime. Her speech was aired anyway. Finally by 1968, Hamer's efforts paid off and she became a member of Mississippi's first integrated delegation to the Democratic National Convention.

That win didn't keep Hamer from challenging other areas that needed reform. For instance, in 1964, she brought hundreds of Black and White college students together to form Freedom Summer, in which the students helped register Black voters in the South. She also announced her campaign for the Mississippi House of Representatives but was kept from the ballot. The next year, she, Victoria Gray, and Annie Devine became the first Black women to stand in US Congress as they protested the 1964 Mississippi House election.

Although her tours around the country speaking about civil rights kept her busy, she still managed to found the National Women's Political Caucus and the Freedom Farm Cooperative which allowed Black people to own and farm collectively. With the help of funds from donors including singer-actor-activist Harry Belafonte, she bought 640 acres to set up a co-op store, sewing business, and boutique. The cooperative also made it possible for two hundred low-income housing units to be built, many of which are still around today. Her cooperative was one of the largest employers Sunflower County, Mississippi, had until the mid-1970s. Hamer herself died not too long after that, in 1977, from breast cancer.

Martyrs of the Movement

We started the chapter with the story of Claudette Colvin being ghosted by the NAACP for being an unwed teen mother. Despite being the most notable person to challenge Montgomery's segregation law before Rosa Parks, her status made her an outcast. In a way, she was a sacrifice made by the civil rights movement. Colvin in action did push the movement forward, but she had to give up a portion of her life, as her reputation was run through the mud.

Thankfully, Colvin was able to keep her life. There were thousands of martyrs in Black America's struggle for equality, including the **4,400 people** who were lynched, drowned, burned, or shot in the South as a result of Jim Crow laws up to about 1950. Those men, women, and children are thankfully now honored at Montgomery's National Memorial for Peace and Justice, spearheaded by the founder of the Equal Justice Initiative (EJI) and public interest lawyer **Bryan Stevenson**. Stevenson's career can be seen as a bridge between the civil rights movement's past and its present, seeing how he has constantly brought his activism into the courtroom and the public sphere with the EJI. His museum dedicated to the thousands of souls lost to racist violence brings their stories back to life and honors them in a way that reminds us that the fight is not over.

While too many of the martyrs in our march toward civil rights have died with their names unetched in the annals of history, there are also others that became infamous in death, such as **Emmett Till**, the fourteen-year-old boy from Chicago who was killed in 1955 while visiting his relatives in Money, Mississippi. Four days after Till was wrongfully accused of flirting with a White woman, the woman's husband and brother tortured Till. They made him carry a seventy-five-pound cotton gin fan to the Tallahatchie riverbank where he was made to take off his clothes; the two men beat him, gouged out one of his eyes, shot him in the head, tied his body to the fan with barbed wire, and threw the boy in the river. When his body was recovered, he was nearly unrecognizable. His mother, **Mamie Till**, ordered for her son to have an open casket funeral so people could see what racial violence had done to her boy's life and image. The gruesome images of Till's disfigured face were published in *JET*, a magazine we will learn more about later in the book. The photographs rocked the nation, especially the pockets of people who had trouble recognizing that the horrors Black Americans were fighting against were real.

Medgar Evers is another casualty of the movement. A civil rights leader in Mississippi, Evers and his family were constantly fighting for their lives amid attacks on their home and personhood. Evers and his family were lucky at first, avoiding a firebomb attack on their home. Despite this, Evers was shot in the back in his own driveway by White supremacist Byron De La Beckwith. He was pronounced dead at the local hospital less than thirty minutes later. It was this tragedy that led his brother and fellow activist, **Charles Evers**, to take over Medgar's spot within the NAACP as state field secretary for Mississippi. Charles was elected mayor of Fayette, Mississippi, in 1969, making him the first Black mayor of a racially mixed Southern town since Reconstruction.

Medgar's widow, **Myrlie Evers-Williams**, also became an important leader within the NAACP. She was elected as the organization's chairwoman of the board of directors in 1995 and kept her post until 1998.

But her achievements within the organization probably pale in comparison to her personal achievements in honoring her late husband's memory and avenging his death. She was the prime force behind getting Medgar's killer charged and put behind bars. Thankfully, her persistence paid off in the 1990s, when Beckwith was arrested. Even though he had been arrested for Medgar's murder before, this time was different, since he was finally convicted by a mixed-race jury. Evers-Williams has kept her late husband's memory alive in another way—by establishing the Medgar Evers Institute in Jackson, the place Evers gave his life for. The institute was later renamed the Medgar and Myrlie Evers Institute to honor the work and sacrifice Myrlie herself endured during the civil rights movement. She currently serves as the institute's chairwoman.

The murder of Selma civil rights activist **Jimmie Lee Jackson** was the catalyst for the marches from Selma to Montgomery. In life, Jackson was a deacon and activist who also served his country in the Vietnam

War before coming back home to injustice in his own state. After he, his grandfather **Cager Lee**, and his mother **Viola Lee Jackson** were turned away from registering to vote in his hometown of Marion in 1962, Jackson became involved in fighting for voting rights. He participated in all manner of protests and boycotts and attended meetings, leading him toward his tragic death.

Marches in both Selma and Marion ended with brutal results. For instance, in Marion, seven thousand children were arrested for marching, and, in Selma, during a march of over three thousand people, civil rights leader **C.T. Vivian** was clubbed and arrested by Selma's Sheriff Jim Clark. The latter event led Vivian to lead another march in Marion. The night march took place February 18 in 1965 with over two hundred people taking part. State troopers and Marion's police chief ordered the group to break up, and after a Black minister was struck by a trooper marchers quickly panicked and began running for shelter. Jackson and his mother ran into Mack's Café when they saw Lee stagger in, bleeding from being beaten. Jackson tried to get his grandfather to a hospital, but they were caged in by troopers and marchers alike. A trooper struck Viola, and Jackson tried to take down the trooper, but his heroism led to his death—the trooper clubbed him and knocked him against a cigarette machine, and another trooper shot Jackson in the stomach. He died at Selma's Good Samaritan Hospital eight days after the attack. Jackson sacrificed his life for the right to vote, so if you're on the fence about voting, consider Jackson's life the next time you think about not casting your ballot.

My hometown of Birmingham also had its share of sacrifices. The most famous martyrs from my city are **Denise McNair**, **Addie Mae Collins**, **Cynthia Wesley**, and **Carole Robertson**, otherwise known to the world as the "four little girls." On a fateful Sunday in September of 1963, they were preparing for a church service in the basement restroom of the 16th Street Baptist Church in downtown Birmingham. A bomb went off. Most of the damage was done in that basement, where the girls were killed.

They weren't the only children to be affected by the blast. One other girl, **Sarah Collins**, Addie Mae's sister, was also with the girls during the bombing. Sarah managed to survive but lost her right eye. Riots broke out in response to the attack, and, as a result, two more children, **Virgil Ware** and **Johnny Robinson**, were killed. On the whole, over twenty others were injured either from the blast or the riots.

Living in a place like Birmingham allows you to never be too far removed from history. Even though the events of the church are now in the past, the church itself is still open for Sunday service. Several of the girls' family members still reside in the city as well, a stark reminder that while the girls' lives have become simply a part of American history, they are still lost loved ones bereaved by their family members first.

Children of the Movement

Emmett Till, the four girls killed at the 16th Street Baptist Church and the two boys killed later that day are only a fraction of the toll children took during the civil rights movement. As the National Memorial for Peace and Justice tells us, there are plenty of children who were killed whose names and stories have been lost to history. It's a shame, since the only way we can learn from the past is if we are able to acknowledge the crimes that have taken place. Thankfully, the memorial can fill in some of those gaps.

Even though the museum has been able to catalogue an impressive 4,400 lives, I wonder how many more have fallen through the gaps of time, not by any fault of the memorial's research team, but because of America's lack of recognition of these lives in the first place. Keep in mind that between the late 1800s all the way up to the early 1960s, Black men, women, and children could be tortured and lynched for a host of reasons—false accusations of rape and murder, trying to vote, talking back to White people, etc.—in front of a crowd of White people, including families with children, at picnic-like fetes. The events would also be money-earners; postcards would be sold with the gruesome images of Black death on the front amid an otherwise idyllic pastoral scene of family "fun."

Who knows how many children's lives have been destroyed by the violence of White supremacy in America. But while Black American children have been subjected to horrors unimaginable to their White counterparts, they've also showcased tremendous courage, sometimes more courage than the adults in their lives.

One such child is **Ruby Bridges**, who became the first Black student to integrate a Southern elementary school. Even though *Brown v. the Board of Education of Topeka, Kansas*, had established integrated schools as the law of the land by the 1950s, Southern schools were still segregated. Bridges tested the Southern resistance against national law when she was enrolled in a segregated kindergarten class in William Frantz Elementary School in New Orleans, her home since she was two years old after her parents moved from Mississippi.

Every morning, Bridges and her mother were escorted by federal marshals to protect them from racist crowds that would heckle them. She spent the entire school year in a classroom by herself after White parents took their kids out of her class. Her parents and grandparents also faced hardship, with her father losing his job and her grandparents being evicted from the farm where they worked and lived as sharecroppers for twenty-five years. However, her courage paved the way for other Black students to enroll. Her bravery not only affected New Orleans, but schools across the South and the entire nation. After the death of her brother Malcolm, Ruby created the Ruby Bridges Foundation in 1999 to promote acceptance and tolerance of others through education.

Other children who moved the needle during the height of the civil rights movement include the children who participated in the **Children's Crusade of 1963**. I mentioned how Shuttlesworth's legacy helped Birmingham become what it is today. But I have to say that the children who participated in the Children's Crusade left a mark that is even more personal since they were willing to put their futures on the line. It's easy to understand how an adult can rationalize the life-and-death risk of standing up for what's good; it's haunting to realize that children were contemplating the same risk, sometimes against the wishes of their understandably scared parents.

The children were part of a plan developed by the SCLC to desegregate Birmingham as a whole, including parks and fairgrounds which only allowed Black youth and families on "colored days."

To be clear, the SCLC's **James Bevel** came up with the idea of utilizing children in a march, and those children, counted in the thousands, were trained on the same tactics of nonviolence that adults had been using throughout the movement.

Not everyone within the civil rights movement were onboard with Bevel's idea. Many were worried about putting kids in harm's way.

Indeed, the threat of harm was real; the first day of the crusade, hundreds of children were arrested. When that didn't deter the crusade, Bull O'Connor, the infamous Commissioner of Public Safety who has gone down in history as one of the most notoriously racist public servants in Birmingham, ordered water hoses sprayed on the children, knocking them down. The children were also battered with police batons and attacked by police dogs, resulting in countless injuries. But the crusade continued, and the images pouring out of Birmingham filled the newspapers around the country.

The gamble of recruiting children was probably one of the riskiest made during the civil rights movement. But the risk paid off; around the country, people were wondering how could a city, much less a region, hate a race so much that it would try to injure and kill children? Public pressure heightened as the children continued the crusade, with one of their last marches taking place to the Birmingham jail where many of their comrades were still in custody.

After being shamed by the enduring national anger, Birmingham officials finally met with the civil rights leaders to desegregate the city. But Birmingham still tried to stick it to the children when the Board of Education decided to expel all of the children who had participated in the crusade. The decision was eventually overturned by the court of appeals.

The entire crusade took place in May of 1963, months before the four girls were killed in the 16th Street Baptist Church bombing. I'm sure at the time, it might have felt like everything the children endured in the crusade was for naught. It probably seemed like Birmingham would never get any better. But we can see the effects of the Children's Crusade today; Birmingham is what it is now because of their personal sacrifice and bravery. If those kids didn't put their lives on the line, my life in Birmingham would certainly be less safe than it is now. In short, all of us in Birmingham, as well as the rest of nation, owe those children a debt of gratitude for their accomplishments and their grace under fire.

Everyday Heroes

There is another batch of unsung heroes that deserve the spotlight: the everyday people who did what they could to participate in the movement. These people, collectively called **foot soldiers**, were numerous and consisted of men and women from all walks of life. You didn't have to be someone with multiple degrees or a pulpit to be part of the movement. All you had to do was take part in the grassroots movement by marching, protesting, boycotting, or otherwise making it known that segregation would stand no longer.

As a Birminghamian, I've grown up with the knowledge of the foot soldiers. I think I've become even more adept at recognizing their accomplishments as I get older, particularly now that I know that so many of them are still alive within the city today. One of them, in fact, works regularly as a substitute teacher at our local fine arts high school—that's how close I am (and others in the city are) to this living history. Birmingham has honored these courageous people, and with good reason, since they helped make the city one of the most progressive places in the South (in my own opinion).

The Results of the Movement

The civil rights movement of the 1950s and 1960s wasn't that long ago—for context, Ruby Bridges is in her sixties today. That means that in the span of a lifetime, a generation of special individuals took the work that had been done by generations before and accelerated it, shaping the country we have today. It's still not a perfect union, but it's much more enjoyable and safer for us Black Americans than it once was just over sixty years ago. However, as the often stated and sometimes cliched saying goes, even though we've come very far, it's clear we still have a long ways to go.

However, what the civil rights leaders and foot soldiers accomplished, all while battling their own differences, should give us hope for what we can achieve today. We don't have to be perfect to strive for a perfect ideal. We can still reach the sky if we aim to touch the stars. To paraphrase King himself, we might not get to the promised land, but we can certainly get closer to it than we believe is possible.

Black Liberal Arts

Clearly, the times featured so far in this book, spanning over two hundred years, weren't the happiest of times for Black Americans. However, while history paints a picture of perpetual doom and gloom, Black Americans still found a way to release stress and tension through the arts.

The arts, such as writing, visual arts, dance, and drama have always had a space in the African diaspora. When speaking about slaves in America specifically, the arts took on even more importance. For those working in the fields and enduring unspeakable crimes, artistic expression (song and dance specifically) became a way of communicating and poking fun at their masters. For instance, the songs that we now call "Negro Spirituals" were created in an effort to keep up morale, but, most importantly, they were codes to other slaves about escape routes. The most popular of these is "Follow the Drinking Gourd," which was first published in 1928, but had supposedly been around since the 1800s and used as instructions for safe passage through the Underground Railroad. The "drinking gourd" (the utensil slaves used to drink water from while on the plantation) was code for the Big Dipper, which pointed toward the North Star and freedom. Both states where slavery was abolished and Canada could be reached by following that star.

Other Negro Spirituals that included secret code were "Swing Low, Sweet Chariot" and "The Gospel Train." They both served Underground Railroad refugees as an oral map about where to go next. Both refer to "stations" on the secretive path to freedom, with "Swing Low, Sweet Chariot" specifically referencing a place on top of a hill by the Ohio River called Ripley. To reach Ripley, a person on the railroad would have to wait for help, which is referenced in the line about the singer looking over Jordan to see "a band of angels" coming to carry them home.

"Wade in the Water," which many probably think of as strictly a Christian song instead of one with a double meaning, is indeed another example of slaves utilizing Christian themes to tell covert messages. **Harriet Tubman**, for instance, used Negro Spirituals as clues to

Harriet Tubman

Black Heritage USA 13c

refugee slaves in her care to follow. The instructions in the song "Wade in the Water" is right there in the title—staying in bodies of water, like rivers or streams, would keep slavecatchers' dogs from sniffing out their scent. Therefore, while the song on the surface sounds like Christian baptism, it is actually telling of a baptism of another sort—a journey from enslavement to freedom.

Tubman and others constantly used spirituals as codes for other slaves, and what's darkly hilarious to me is that slaveowners seemed to not catch on to what slaves were doing. Yes, some slaveowners differed in what they would allow their slaves to sing. But generally, "Christian"-based work songs were seen as okay since, to the slaveowner, it showed that the slaves were being indoctrinated into Western religion (and therefore had their souls "saved" by their White masters). The songs also allowed slaves to use their masters' racism in their favor. While the master might have thought their slaves were happily (and mindlessly) singing about Jesus Christ, the slaves were, in fact, having an entire conversation about escape routes, tactics and strategy in broad daylight, and no one was the wiser.

The same thing happened with dance, such as the Cakewalk. The Cakewalk, which earned its name from plantation contests in which the prize was an extravagantly decorated cake, was developed by slaves as a way to make fun of their masters. The dance was mimicking a promenade of sorts that the White gentry would do at balls. The dancers' demeanor was all a front, poking fun at the White elite's focus on gentility, an irony seeing how White supremacy was responsible for some serious human rights atrocities. The hilariously embellished dance, however, was a small way the slaves could get back at their slaveowners.

Ironically, the plantation owners often were judges during the Cakewalk contests, clearly not getting that the dances they were judging were poking direct jabs at them. The Cakewalk was "playing the dozens" in dancing form, a brilliant way of undercutting White supremacy's power in an unexpected way.

Seeing how integral song and dance were to Black Americans way back when, it makes sense to me as to why so much of African American culture is intertwined with the arts. These examples show how the arts in general have been used as our weapons, our protection, and for our cultural touchstones.

Musical Pioneers

There are plenty of early Black musicians that we know by name, but there are some that we don't, like the slaves who invented the blues, the basis of most pop music today. No one person invented the blues; it was the collective inventiveness of slaves and sharecroppers that developed the style from the songs they'd sing while working on the plantations, with the genre's roots grounded in various influences such as African chants and spirituals, drumming, field hollers, Southern-style revivalist music and more. The genre stayed in the southern part of the US until the 1930s and 1940s, when it moved to the Midwest and elsewhere, branching off into different regional styles of blues.

Even though no one person created the blues, bandleader and songwriter **W.C. Handy** is credited with bringing blues to the mainstream. He is also credited as saying that he learned about jazz in Mississippi from a street guitarist in 1903. Handy was originally from the South himself; he was born in Florence, Alabama, to former slaves. His uncle, also an ex-slave, earned a reputation as a fiddler while on

the plantation, and Handy's family's love for music influenced him to start his music career.

After learning of the blues in Mississippi, he later moved his family to Memphis, Tennessee, and began writing blues pieces, such as "Memphis Blues," which he self-published in 1912. His most famous work, "Saint Louis Blues," was published in 1914 with businessman and lyricist **Harry Pace**. This song became Handy's claim to fame, and it's reported that twenty-five years after the song was released, it was still raking in twenty-five thousand dollars in yearly royalties. That's what you call a hit.

While W.C. Handy hit it big with "Saint Louis Blues," **Gertrude "Ma" Rainey** is known as the "Mother of the Blues." As someone born in Georgia with parents from Alabama, she had the country blues in her blood, and she started performing at the early age

of fourteen. She married William Rainey later in her teenage years, and together they both toured with the Rabbit Foot Minstrels.

Even though Handy is credited as making the blues mainstream, I wonder if that's because of male privilege. Why? If we go by some of the research, Rainey might have sang the blues while with the minstrel troupe. If so, that means she was singing to crowds in the style of the genre a whole seventeen years before the big blues takeover in the 1910s! So even though Rainey is given the honor of being called the "Mother of Blues," maybe she should get even more credit for what she's done for bringing the genre to the masses.

It was during her time with the Rabbit Foot Minstrels that Rainey mentored a young **Bessie Smith**, who would later earn the title of the "Empress of Blues" in her career for her charismatic acts and songs. She became the highest-paid Black performer of her time, not only making her a Black musical great, but also a boundary-breaker for LGBT Black performers. Smith was married to security guard Jack Gee and later on had a common-law marriage to a friend, Richard Morgan. But throughout her rocky relationship with Gee, she had various relationships with women while Gee was also having affairs. It's even rumored that Smith and Rainey had a relationship even though there's no evidence to back up this assumption.

Regardless, Smith was a woman who didn't hide who she was. In fact, she was open about her sexuality in songs such as "It's Dirty but Good," in which she sang, "I know women that don't like men."

She was a performer who lived hard and loud, and, even in death, she courted controversy. When she was killed in 1937 in Mississippi from injuries in a car accident, the manner of her death was mired in questions, such as whether her injuries were ignored because of her race. Most historians believe that Smith's injuries were still mortal wounds and she would have died regardless. Ultimately, we'll never know the truth.

 While Ma Rainey is the Mother of Blues, **Sister Rosetta Tharpe** is considered the Godmother of Rock and Roll. Tharpe created the genre by blurring together gospel, jazz, and blues with her signature talent as a guitarist. She broke into fame in 1938 with her song "Rock Me," which was shocking for its sexual content mixed with its gospel-esque sound. She traveled around the country in the 1930s and 1940s, singing gospel and utilizing her own rock and roll sound. She is credited as having the first gospel crossover hit with her 1945 "Strange Things Happening Every Day." This

crossover led to the origins of mainstream Rhythm and Blues but also became a blueprint for modern rock and roll.

Like Smith, Tharpe was also a bisexual icon, having relationships with men and women as well as several marriages. She even toured with her partner Marie Knight as a duo with their own band. But Tharpe's career as an early rock and roll pioneer waned in the 1950s when the genre started becoming synonymous with young White guys like the Rolling Stones, The Beatles, and, the most controversial of them all, Elvis Presley. But she still toured throughout Europe, garnering huge crowds. She kept her career alive overseas until she died in 1973. But Tharpe's influence kept going beyond her death due to one other action earlier in her career. In 1947, she discovered a fourteen-year-old boy and put him on stage. That boy, Richard Penniman, later became known as **Little Richard**, one of the greatest rock and roll performers of the 1950s and a queer icon in his own right.

Jackie Shane builds on the status Smith and Tharpe created by becoming a pioneering transgender soul singer in North America. Shane was born in Nashville, Tennessee, but she established her career in Toronto, Canada. She became huge there, performing for large crowds in nightclubs and eventually for TV on the Toronto show *Night Train*. Her performances on the show were for integrated audiences, furthering her power in the R&B industry.

However, her career fell out of the public eye after 1971, leaving many to believe she had died. Others, like me, had never even heard of her until recently. However, her reason for staying away from the limelight was personal. As she told the *New York Times*, she stopped her career to take care of her mother in Los Angeles. After her mother died, she moved back to Nashville. But her career was brought back into full scope in 2017 when record label Numero Group released her music on a boxed set called *Any Other Way*. It was nominated for a Grammy for Best Historical Album, cementing Shane's musical legacy.

She died in 2019, and I wish America had embraced her earlier in her career the same way Toronto did; while we in America have little to no knowledge of Shane, she is so legendary in Toronto that her visage is on a mural with other R&B, blues, and rockabilly greats.

I'm a huge disco fan, so while I can't feature every Black disco group or singer that made the genre one of Afrocentrism and self-affirmation, I must talk about at least one singer, the iconic **Sylvester.** Born Sylvester James Jr., he is one of the most interesting and singular disco and R&B singers of the late seventies and eighties (and one of my favorites).

One of the few openly gay artists during the late 1970s and 1980s, Sylvester carved out his own lane with his androgynous fashion sense and vocal stylings directly influenced by the Black church. His gospel infusion into disco led to some of his biggest hits (and some of my personal favorites) such as "You Make Me Feel (Mighty Real)" and "Dance (Disco Heat)."

Sylvester, nicknamed the "Queen of Disco," was always proud of himself, despite rampant homophobia during the seventies and eighties, and gave his audience permission to embrace themselves or others who might be different from them. He also used his fame to propel his activism, which included fighting against the spread of HIV/AIDS through the eighties. Unfortunately, Sylvester became one of the casualties of the virus, dying in 1988. But he still used his star power to help those in need for generations to come; in his will, he left all his future royalties to California-based HIV/AIDS charity Project Open Hand and the AIDS Emergency Fund.

Dance Revolutionaries

As much as I love dance, I'd never cried during a ballet performance until I saw the **Alvin Ailey** dance troupe. To me, it is just one example of how Alvin Ailey's influence as a dancer and African American storyteller still lives on.

Ailey changed the dance world forever when he created the Alvin Ailey American Dance Theater in 1958. The company, still in existence today, brings together dancers from different races to bring modern dance to poetic heights. Its most popular work is Ailey's *Revelations*, which draws from Ailey's own Southern Black upbringing, which includes the Black church services he attended as a child.

Ailey was living his truth as a dancer early in his life. At just twelve years old, Ailey left his home state of Texas for Los Angeles. It was this move that put him in the path of the Ballet Russe de Monte Carlo. He was inspired to become a dancer and began studying under modern dance pioneer Lester Horton, the man credited with creating the first integrated dance company in America.

His tutelage under Horton led him to Broadway in Truman Capote's musical *House of Flowers* and other musicals such as *The Carefree Tree* and *Jamaica*, which starred Black actress, singer, and activist **Lena Horne** and Ricardo Montalban. But it's what Ailey did the year after *Jamaica* that launched him into the stratosphere of dance. That year, 1958, Ailey launched his own dance company. Ailey's talents also caught the eye of the US State Department, who sponsored his company's tour in the 1960s. In 1969, he created another gem in his legacy, the Alvin Ailey American Dance Center, now known as the Ailey School.

Ailey choreographed nearly eighty ballets throughout his career and was honored by the Kennedy Center in 1988 for his contributions to the arts. This accolade was a beautiful bookend for his career, because, unfortunately, Ailey died in December of the following year from AIDS (originally, his death was attributed to "terminal blood dyscrasia" by *The New York Times*).

Janet Collins, like Ailey, made it possible for Black American expression to take hold in the world of ballet. Collins faced backlash when she attempted to enter ballet. She tried to audition for the Ballet Russe de Monte Carlo at fifteen years old but was told she would have to disguise her race. She could have taken the offer as someone with "passing" privilege, but thankfully she declined and made it in ballet her own way. Her journey toward stardom with integrity paid off when she was awarded the Donaldson Award for

Best Broadway dancer for her role in Cole Porter's *Out of this World*. In 1951, she joined the Metropolitan Opera and, a year later, she became the company's first Black prima ballerina. She also passed on her knowledge to other dancers as a modern dance teacher at the School of American Ballet and at Manhattanville College.

Misty Copeland is one of today's ballet dancers making waves with this generation's group of Black dancers. I first saw her perform with **Prince** on George Lopez's now-defunct late-night talk show, *Lopez Tonight*.

Copeland made history as the first Black woman to be named the principal dancer for the American Ballet Theater, a feat that is both impressive and sobering, seeing how long ballet has been a part of the American landscape. However, if you're familiar with ballet, you'll know that colorism and racism have both played an unfortunately big role in the industry. Case in point: only recently have pointe shoes been made in different flesh tones.

Sadly, Copeland hasn't been immune to racism, not just in the world of ballet, but even in her own personal life. Her mother's fourth husband was physically and emotionally abusive, calling his stepchildren and wife racial slurs. Thankfully, Copeland was able to purge much of her anxiety in dance, first by finding common ground with the story of famed gymnast Nadia Comaneci and creating dance routines based on Mariah Carey songs. She became the captain of her middle school drill team, and, at the behest of her teacher, she began taking ballet at her Boys and Girls Club. Her teacher, Cynthia Bradley, quickly realized Copeland was a prodigy.

Bradley became more than just her teacher. After Copeland's mother left her husband and moved her family into a motel, she decided to let Copeland live with Bradley so she could continue her dance lessons. Copeland's biggest moments in her teenage career included important performances such as a charity event featuring Angela Bassett and with Debbie Allen's production of *The Chocolate Nutcracker*.

Her tumultuous family life became even more so by this point, leading Copeland to consider emancipating herself from her mother after she was ordered to come back home. Copeland kept dancing despite the setbacks. She joined the American Ballet Theater in 2000 and began rising to the top of the company toward her top spot today.

She is probably the most notable dancer to most people who don't keep up with the dance world simply because she's crossed over from the insular dance world to mainstream pop culture. Her activism comes through her dance and her personhood; she's someone who probably would have been passed over, if we go by conventional statistics about what makes a child successful. Instead, through the help of a mentor, she was able to rise from a childhood of confusion to reach her fullest potential. She has defied the odds and was one of *Time* magazine's 100 Most

Influential People in 2015; recently, Barbie awarded her with her very own doll as part of the Shero collection. In fact, she's been turned into a Barbie twice over with another doll based on her character in Disney's 2018 holiday film *The Nutcracker and the Four Realms*.

Journalist Role Models

I can't leave journalists out of this chapter! I'm an author right now, but when I'm not writing a book, I'm living life as an entertainment journalist. While entertainment is my main love, I've worked in "hard news" journalism—politics, social issues, and more—as much as I have in the more fun realms of the industry. Regardless of what branch of journalism I'm doing, I have several pioneers to thank. Without them, it would have been infinitely harder for me to do what I love.

The first Black newspaper in America was ***Freedom's Journal***, created by **Samuel Eli Cornish**, abolitionist, editor, and minister, and **John Russwurm**, a Jamaican-born Canadian who later moved to Maine to attend Bowdoin College, becoming the second person of African descent in America to earn a college degree. His graduation speech, much like his field of study, focused on the Haitian Revolution and its leader Toussaint L'Ouverture, which should give you an inkling of how revolutionary his and Cornish's newspaper would end up being.

The newspaper not only spoke to its Black audience about issues of the day, but it also took direct shots at White newspapers such as the *New York Enquirer*, whose publisher Mordecai Noah took specific delight in talking smack about freed Blacks. Even though the paper was a godsend to abolitionists and kept African American readers informed and enlightened about their environment, the paper sadly came to an end two years later due to disagreements between Cornish and Russwurm over the subject of African Americans colonizing Africa. However, during its time in the sun, *Freedom's Journal* was popular throughout the country, with its circulation extending to eleven states and Washington DC, Haiti, Canada, and Europe.

Ida B. Wells-Barnett, otherwise known as simply Ida B. Wells, was one of the great journalists and activists of the late 1800s and early 1900s. She was born into slavery during the Civil War in Mississippi, but, after the war, her parents became politically active, which was probably the beginning of Wells-Barnett's own interest in politics and social justice. She was expelled from Rust College after starting an argument with the university's president, but this also exemplified her tireless and bold search for the truth that characterized her career.

Sadly, her parents and her brother were killed by yellow fever, so, as a young adult, she had to take care of her remaining siblings by working as a teacher. Even after her family's move to Memphis, Tennessee, she kept teaching until she filed a lawsuit against a Memphis train company for throwing her off a train despite her first-class ticket. Although she won the case locally, the ruling was overturned federally. This, combined with one of her friends being lynched, led Wells toward a life of reporting on the injustice around her. She investigated several lynchings of Black men in the community and released her findings in newspaper columns and pamphlets.

Her work exposing the corruption in the town put her and her family in danger, and she had to relocate to Chicago. However, this didn't stop her from reporting the truth. She continued her activism and traveled around the world, calling boycotts, bringing attention to lynchings, and confronting White suffragettes for ignoring the human cost of lynching. Because she dared to confront them with their own injustice, she was often left out of women's rights organizations. But she kept fighting for women's rights by starting the National Association of Colored Women's Club and was in Niagara Falls at the founding of the NAACP; however, she's not listed as an official member. Regardless, Wells fought for freedom her own way, with her words and sheer will.

Clarence O. Smith and **John H. Johnson**'s names should be familiar to us, since they started the Black-centric magazines *Essence* and *Ebony*. Smith cofounded *Essence* with Edward Lewis in 1970, right at the height of a sea change in America. This was the point where Blackness was finally beginning to be recognized and accepted, thanks to the civil rights movement. This newly empowered group of consumers, including Black women, needed something that would reach them where they were—women who were going after the American dream, fighting for their rights, and trying to look and feel good while doing it.

Smith and Lewis attracted huge advertisers to the magazine, leading *Essence* to become one of the

CHAPTER 4: BLACK LIBERAL ARTS

most prominent magazines in America. Smith in particular took the brand even further by establishing The Essence Awards television special and other licensing opportunities.

Johnson, Like Smith and Lewis, established *Ebony* and its sister publication *Jet* in order to reflect a sophisticated African American market. *Ebony* wasn't Johnson's first publication—his first ever was *Negro Digest*, later renamed *Black World*, which utilized the format of *Reader's Digest*. But *Ebony*, created in 1945, is undoubtedly his most famous creation, which paved the way for its sister publication *Jet*, which launched in 1951. *Ebony* has set the bar high for other magazines in its market—*Ebony* has been the top African American magazine since its first year, and *Jet* has become the world's biggest Black weekly magazine. Johnson, like Smith, also pushed his business into new territory, starting ventures such as beauty line Fashion Fair, which catered specifically to Black women who were underserved in the market. He also produced television specials and, in a twist of fate, became the chairman and CEO of the place where he started his career, Supreme Life Insurance.

Gwen Ifill became the first Black woman to host a nationally televised political talk show when she served as the managing editor and moderator of PBS's news show *Washington Week* as well as *The PBS NewsHour*'s senior political correspondent in 1999. This was the cherry on top of an illustrious career starting at the *Boston Herald* newspaper in 1977. She worked at several newspapers throughout the eighties, including the *Baltimore Evening Sun* and the *Washington*

Post before moving on to work as a White House correspondent for the *New York Times* in 1991. Her time as White House correspondent can be seen as a shift between her time as a printed journalist toward her time as a journalist on screen, since, in 1994, she began working with NBC News. Her tenure as the network's chief congressional and political correspondent was just right for her career with PBS, where complete and thorough reporting is key to putting out trustworthy news to a discerning audience.

Her career is filled with awards, including a Peabody Award, highly coveted in the world of journalism, as well as a Leonard Zeidenberg First Amendment Award. Sadly, Ifill's career was cut short by a battle with endometrial cancer, and she died in 2012 at the age of sixty-one. However, she left behind an entire generation of journalists, particularly women of color, inspired by her presence on screen and in print throughout their lives.

Like Ifill, **Lester Holt** also made television history when he became the first Black host of *NBC Nightly News* in 2015. Holt's start in journalism was rocky; he dropped out of college to work at a radio station in his hometown of San Francisco. Two years later, he began working with CBS as a reporter for a CBS affiliate in New York City. Little did he know that this job would launch him into a nineteen-year career with CBS with jobs in New York, Los Angeles, and Chicago.

After his CBS career, Holt joined MSNBC in 2000 as a substitute anchor for *NBC Nightly News* and *Today*. He was later made the *Nightly News* weekend anchor until 2015, when he made history as the weekday

Nightly News host. Holt's transition to the job was probably a jolt to many viewers, who had seen Brian Williams in the position for years. But Williams was in trouble for making several factually inaccurate statements about events he reported on, so his sudden vacancy made sense. (As to why he's back on TV at MSNBC is a different story entirely and could be the subject of its own book.) Holt took the role and returned it to the dignified position it once had before Williams's scandal.

Tamron Hall is one of my favorite journalists and I aspire to align myself with her. Hall is an award-nominated and -winning journalist who is best known for her former anchor role on MSNBC's *NewsNation* and *Today*. She left NBC in 2017 and is now working on her new daytime talk show, which airs across the nation.

Hall's work expands beyond her journalism; she uses her profile to advocate more interest in cold cases and domestic violence, due to a personal connection. Her sister died as a result of domestic violence, in a case that, unfortunately, remains unsolved. Hall is an example of how to use one's platform and talents to shine a light on issues in the world.

Artistic Pioneers

I started out life as an artist. Art is one of the ways I've been able to practice self-expression, and my life has been thoroughly enriched by it. Even though I'm currently not making a living as a visual artist, my work and the work of others have plenty of earlier artists to thank. While we often think of people like Monet and Picasso when we consider art, there are a lot of creative forefathers and foremothers who don't get enough recognition.

Visual art legends can come from anywhere. That fact has never been truer than with the **Gee's Bend Quilters**, a group of Black women from Alabama who have created some of the world's most renown quilts.

The existence of the quilting group in Gee's Bend has been known to the public since the early 1900s. The citizens of Gee's Bend, a little patch of land surrounded by the Alabama River on three sides, are descendants of slaves who worked for the nearby Pettaway plantation. The quilts these artists have created hold within them African American creativity and history, and generations of women have kept the quilting tradition alive.

Carrie Mae Weems is considered to be one of America's most influential contemporary artists. From photography to film, her work investigates the facets of the African American identity. Her art, in which Weems utilized black-and-white photography and photography negatives, frequently showcases her subjects in pared-down settings, highlighting the experience of Blackness as being one of existing in, but never belonging to America's social fabric. Her biggest works throughout her career, *Ain't Joking*, *The Kitchen Table Series*, *From Here I Saw What Happened and I Cried*, *The Louisiana Project*, and *Roaming*, exemplify her interest in investigating the condition of being Black in America. She has also used her art for social justice initiatives such as Operation Activate, an anti-gun violence public art campaign, and the Institute of Sound and Style, which gives kids the chance to gain training in visual arts.

Jackie Ormes, America's first Black cartoonist, created characters that brought dignity and style back to the image of the African American. She created her comic strips between the 1930s and 1950s, when Black people were still being depicted as pickaninnies and mammies. Thankfully, her pin-up-esque comics, particularly the one centering on fashionable, glamorous socialite Torchy Brown, provided Black readers a counterpoint to all of the horrible imagery they were receiving about themselves. Ormes was also a dollmaker, turning one of her characters, a precocious little girl named Patty-Jo, into a doll in the late 1940s. What Ormes did with Patty-Jo was a feat during a time when the majority of dolls on the market were White and the ones that were Black were seen as ugly. Ormes's career in general was a boon for those growing up who wanted to see themselves living the upper-crust life.

Gordon Parks is one of the greatest photographers to document Black life in America. Parks's love for photography began in his young adulthood when he saw black and white dramatic images of migrant workers in a magazine. He bought his camera at a pawn shop and learned how to use it. He was talented—even though he had no professional photography experience, he was able to secure a job with the Farm Security Administration (FSA) to take photo evidence of various social issues such as the devastation of The Great Depression.

After the FSA closed in 1943, Parks had to find work as a fashion photographer until *Life* editors saw his 1948 photo essay on the life of a Harlem gang leader; the magazine hired him. His position with *Life* made him the first Black staff photographer and writer for the publication, breaking the color line at *Life* and furthering the African American footprint in mainstream photography. He also became huge in Hollywood, becoming the first African American to write and direct a feature film, 1969's *The Learning Tree*, based on Parks's book of the same name. In 1971, he also directed *Shaft*, one of the most iconic blaxploitation films ever.

Black Writers

The first published Black female poet was **Phillis Wheatley**. Wheatley was a slave in the prominent Boston household of John Wheatley. Phillis's origins lay in Senegal and Gambia where she was kidnapped, transported, and sold into service. Even though she was seen as a weak child, she soon became an important part of the Wheatley household and was taught to read and write. Wheatley had an interest in many subjects, such as astronomy, history, British literature, Biblical works, and ancient Latin and Greek works. Her interest in learning is reflected in what is believed to be her first poem, "To the University of Cambridge in New England."

Her first published poem, however, is thought to be "An Elegiac Poem, on the Death of that Celebrated Divine, and Eminent Servant of Jesus Christ, the Reverende and Learned George Whitefield" in 1770. Her poem made her a worldwide superstar, with abolitionists using her as an example to show that African slaves weren't merely chattel—they were people with interests in the arts and creative expression. As an eighteen-year-old, Wheatley had written twenty-eight poems and, after American publishers refused to look at her work, the Wheatleys had her book, *Poems on Various Subjects, Religious and Moral* published in London in 1773, making Phillis the first Black person to have a volume of poetry published in the modern world.

After Wheatley was manumitted in 1773, her troubles were far from over. The Wheatleys began dying off years after her manumission, leaving her alone, despite her marriage to a free Black man: lawyer and entrepreneur, John Peters. He, like Wheatley, lived the life of a genteel person, but Wheatley, Peters, and their children fell into deep debt and Peters was eventually arrested and put in debtor's prison. Wheatley died soon after in 1784. Before her death, despite her ups and downs, Wheatley had continued to write, and her work leaves a legacy that has paved the way for many Black poets to follow.

I never see too much ado about **Octavia E. Butler**, even though she's a cornerstone of modern science fiction. Even if you haven't read any of Butler's works, such as *Patternmaster, Kindred, Fledgling*, and many more, you probably still know of them without realizing it. Why? Because her works constitute what we think of as Afrofuturism, an aesthetic and activist movement that encompasses various forms of art, music, and literature, which intersects Black history and culture with science and/or technology. Afrofuturistic works imagine, investigate, and celebrate alternative futures for Black identity.

Butler did this in her books by imbuing them with themes of African spirituality, such as in her Patternist series starting with *Patternmaster*, in which the characters are telepathically linked to a four-thousand-year-old African immortal named Doro. Other books, such as *Kindred* and *Bloodchild* examine the African American experience of enslavement. Thankfully, her work is now being adapted into television and film projects we will soon be able to binge watch.

Richard Wright documented the experience of being a Black man in America. He was one of the first Black writers to openly skewer White treatment of Black Americans in his 1940 novel *Native Son* and his 1945 autobiography *Black Boy*. Both books and other works by Wright investigate the perils of being Black and male in America, drawing from his own politically charged background and his grandparents' experiences as slaves. The original film adaptation of *Native Son* was made in Argentina in 1951, ten years after Orson Welles brought the book to Broadway. In the 1951 film version, Wright played his book's main character, Bigger Thomas. Now, this generation has our own film version of *Native Son* thanks to HBO, with the role of Bigger Thomas played by Ashton Sanders.

Did you grow up reading **Zora Neale Hurston**'s *Their Eyes Were Watching God* in high school? If you're raising your hand, I'm raising mine  alongside you. I was first introduced to Hurston in tenth grade, and reading her book was a unique experience for me, since I don't think I had read many books written by Black authors by that time aside from American Girl's Addy book collection.

A Notasulga, Alabama, native, Hurston wrote *Their Eyes Were Watching God* not in her home state, but in the midst of the height of the Harlem Renaissance. Whereas Wright related the Black male experience in America, Hurston wrote about the Black female experience, particularly one located in the South. Even though Hurston died in 1960, her work as an anthropologist lives on in the form of a recently released posthumous book, *Barracoon: The Story of the Last "Black Cargo."* This nonfiction book relates the story of a person we met all the way back in Chapter 1—Kudjo Lewis, one of the last slaves brought to America.

Hopefully *Barracoon* will bring to light more of Hurston's anthropological work, which often documented her travels to the South and the Caribbean to document cultural practices of Black locals. She was able to do this work thanks to support from philanthropist Charlotte Osgood Mason and, later, the Guggenheim Foundation and the Federal Writer's Project. Her travels led to her books *Mules and Men* and *Tell My Horse*. Hurston also shot documentary footage as a part of her fieldwork in Haiti and Florida, documenting rare evidence of the Vodou and Hoodoo religion within and outside of America.

Speaking of films, Hurston's *Their Eyes Were Watching God* was turned into a TV movie in 2005 by Oprah Winfrey, starring Halle Berry and Michael Ealy.

Toni Morrison, born Chloe Anthony Wofford, is known around the world for her writings on the experiences of Black women in America. Her books, which include *The Bluest Eye* and *Song of Solomon* among others, examine how Black men and women are often made to negotiate

their Blackness in order to have an identity acceptable to the mainstream. Her writings earned her a Nobel Prize for Literature in 1993. Along with that honor, her work has also been highly sought after in Hollywood, with Oprah Winfrey bringing her Pulitzer Prize-winning book *Beloved* to the big screen. Morrison helped generations of writers hone their crafts by teaching at State University of New York at Albany and Princeton University before retiring in 2006. Morrison also expanded the literary world through her work as Random House's first African American female editor. During her tenure between 1967 and 1983, Morrison brought to the masses the works of Black activists and notables like Muhammad Ali, Huey P. Newton, Gayl Jones, Angela Davis, and others. Her work and her life are still impacting people today, most notably through the 2019 documentary, *Toni Morrison: The Pieces I Am.* Morrison died in 2019 at the age of eighty-eight.

A Creative Legacy

This is only a smattering of people that belong on the "Awesome Black Americans" list. As someone in the liberal arts world myself, I could have filled this entire book with people who have changed the face of America as we know it through their creativity. It's astounding how much America has been shaped by the African American artistic output, even when our ancestors were enslaved and working on the plantations. Somehow, we managed to free ourselves through song, dance, visual arts and the written word.

We stand on the shoulders of many giants in our chosen liberal arts fields. We have to remember that while we might think we have it tough today, our spiritual mentors might consider this a cakewalk (pardon the pun, now that we know what "cakewalk" means). They had it much rougher than we do, with less technology and even less of an ability to "make it," as it were—racism kept many creatives out of venues and away from opportunities. To paraphrase a popular saying, still they persisted. And the fruits of their labor give us the space to realize our biggest, best, and most creative selves.

Beautiful Blackness

Perhaps it's because I have an arts background that makeup has become a new obsession for me. However, if you're like me and you know you love makeup, have you ever taken a look at your personal collection to see how many of these products are from Black-owned businesses?

Similarly, if you love primping your hair, have you ever thought about the types of products you use for your haircare routine? Are they from brands started by Black haircare enthusiasts who wanted to create products that meet the needs of Black and ethnic hair?

Maybe you have a ton of products by Black-created brands, or maybe you are just starting your collection. Regardless, if you're interested in beauty on any level, you have probably realized that Black-owned businesses are on the rise. If I can rework the classic phrase, Black is the new Black when it comes to the fashion and beauty industry.

Unfortunately, it hasn't always been this way—Black beauty hasn't always been en vogue. For decades, America praised Whiteness as the ultimate beauty standard. Thankfully, Black women and men were able to fight their way inside the industries and mold it to their own image. I know I'm personally grateful, because, as another old adage states, when you look good, you feel good. And when you feel good, you can access the confidence and self-esteem you need to conquer the world.

Redefining Beauty

There was a time when it was hard for many Black Americans to come to terms with their identity. I think the best example of that for me are the "doll tests" psychologists **Drs. Kenneth and Mamie Clark** conducted in the 1940s. Black children were given four dolls that were identical except in terms of their skin color. The Clarks asked which doll they preferred and found that most of the Black children chose the White doll, associating it with positive attributes, while the Black doll was instead associated with negative attributes, including ugliness. The children's reactions to the dolls reflected their own image about themselves, taught to them by society at large. The Clarks determined that "prejudice, discrimination, and segregation" created feelings of inferiority and low self-esteem among Black children. Self-esteem was so bad that one child in Arkansas said of the brown doll he was pointing to, "That's a nigger. I'm a nigger." Or, among some children in Massachusetts, Kenneth noted, they "would cry and run out of the room."

Self-esteem is more than just believing you can accomplish something; it's also about seeing yourself as aesthetically pleasing. It's clear many of these children had already internalized negative images of themselves, as seen in the way they described the

Black dolls, but also in the way they described the White dolls. Part of that negative image has to affect standards of beauty: if you see someone more likable, accepted, and as an aspirational figure, you would also see them as more beautiful.

Unfortunately, a bias toward lighter skin still exists if you pay attention to today's media. However, I feel that we have come some distance from where we started—for instance, Black dolls weren't even being produced at the time of the Clarks' original tests, so they had to paint a White doll brown for the experiments. Also, the tests helped influence the outcome of *Brown vs. The Board of Education of Topeka, Kansas,* which rules that racial segregation in public schools was unconstitutional. So movement toward progress does exist.

Thinking of Blackness in terms of beauty has always been a radical, political act in this country ever since slavery embedded itself into the nation's fabric. As you can infer from the background above, there was a time when thinking a Black person was beautiful was potentially laughable. Case in point: the Tignon Laws, the set of rules enacted in New Orleans in the late 1700s that prohibited Black women from showing their hair. As the Tignon Laws illustrate, people were very much aware of Black style, but to admit that a Black person was beautiful was controversial and even indecent. So, it comes as no surprise that the popular saying, "Black is beautiful" has been seen as a revolutionary statement in the past.

Instead, the statement should be interpreted as meaning Black people are just as beautiful as anyone else. A Black person can choose how they want to express themselves regardless of what others say. That's the essence of "Black is beautiful."

John S. Rock is credited with coming up with the phrase "Black is beautiful." He was a Black abolitionist who was also the first Black person to be admitted to the Supreme Court bar. He's supposed to have said a version of "Black is beautiful" during an 1858 speech, and the phrase has been kept alive to this day. In each generation, the phrase takes on a different layer of meaning. In my opinion, during the sixties and seventies and decades beyond, the phrase has been used to signify Black beauty—and the Black Beauty industry—as a political statement.

The Evolution of Black Haircare

If you need a refresher, refer back to the second chapter, where we covered several Black haircare pioneers who changed the game for how Black people took their beauty into their own hands. The lane Black haircare businessowners created gave the everyday Black person a way to express themselves in new and unique ways.

There can be a conversation about how early Black haircare might have perpetuated White Western stereotypes about beauty, such as the ongoing conversation about straightening Black hair to fit into mainstream society versus wearing your hair completely natural. Even within the natural hair community, there is a preference for a certain coily hair type that can easily withstand wash-and-go treatments versus the more tightly coiled hair textures. It's a colorism discussion of hair, if you will, with coily hair seen as more desirable because it's more closely associated with lightness or Whiteness. Again, the remnants of the low self-esteem showcased in the Clarks' doll tests crop up in all manner of ways, including something like hair management. Regardless of what part certain businesses might have had in that conversation, we can acknowledge that these pioneering beauty professionals laid the groundwork for future Black businesses to advance what it means to be Black and beautiful.

There are probably a lot of Black-owned hair companies that have come and gone throughout the decades that we'll never know of. However, even though many companies and their products have died out or were acquired by larger ones over the years, there are a lot from the olden days that are still kicking today. One happens to be products inspired by **Madam C.J. Walker** herself.

The Madam C.J. Walker Beauty Culture line was created by **Richelieu Dennis**, CEO of ethnic haircare company Sundial Brands, and **A'Lelia Bundles**, Walker's great-great-granddaughter. You can either walk into your local Sephora or go to their website and get your own piece of haircare history.

These aren't the only products from Black America's beauty past in demand today. If you grew up with products like Luster's Pink Oil Moisturizer and Blue Magic hair grease in your house, then you grew up with living pieces of history. The next time you're in your bathroom or visiting with relatives and you see Luster's Pink Oil Moisturizer in its proper place on the counter or in the vanity cabinet, think of **Fred Luster.** This Mississippi native moved as a child with his family to Chicago in 1934 and started out his adult career as a steelworker. But his trajectory changed toward business while on strike from his job in 1950. To keep a flow of income during the strike, he started cutting hair. After realizing he had a knack with customers and with cuts, he became a barber, doing haircuts and hair relaxation. He also started creating and selling his own relaxer, cementing his talents even further.

It only took him seven years to generate enough capital to open a plant. He moved his plant from its original address to Michigan Avenue in 1971, where it has grown into the international company it is today.

The best-known product from Luster's company is, of course, the aforementioned Pink Oil Moisturizer. Even though Luster created tons of products for customers, the Pink Oil Moisturizer is what has become synonymous with Black hair hygiene. Luster died in 1991, but his products are still in demand today. Case in point—I have some Pink Oil Moisturizer as part of my own hair supplies. I bought some because I remembered it being a part of my hair routine as a child and the nostalgia factor convinced me to give the product another shot. But I can also say that it's just plain good, at least for my personal hair type. There's a reason why this moisturizer has stuck around for so many years.

Another product ubiquitous with Black American haircare is Blue Magic pressing oil, or as you probably grew up calling it, Blue Magic hair grease, because, let's be honest—Blue Magic is like blue Crisco for your hair.

Even though I'm making jokes, Blue Magic was one of the premier products for Black hairstyling. The brand continues to be popular with hairstylists because of its long history and reliable results. As one of its vintage ads stated, it "reconditions hair [and] helps dry scalp, helps prevent burning" during the hair straightening process, "gives lovely, high silky gloss" and "hold[s] hair longer for [a] lasting, natural look." Having experienced Blue Magic myself growing up, I can vouch for all of this. As with Luster's Pink Oil Moisturizer, I also have some Blue Magic in my arsenal because of the nostalgia factor—I know how to work with it because my mother used it on my hair all the time. And it actually works when you want moisturizer with some staying power.

Blue Magic was manufactured by J. Strickland & Co., founded by **George B. Long.** Long went into the haircare business in 1936 when he borrowed five hundred dollars as seed money. While Blue Magic is probably his best-known product, it wasn't created until 1968. Instead, Long's first products were Royal Crown Hair Dressing and White Rose Petroleum Jelly.

The industry has changed a lot since Blue Magic and Luster's Pink Hair Conditioner first hit the market. In fact the industry was changing even as those two products were at the height of their popularity. When the mid-sixties and early 1970s rolled in, so did natural hairstyling. Thanks to the civil rights movement and its spiritual cousin the Black Power movement, natural hairstyles such as afros and braids became en vogue. It was a celebration of Black hair without any alterations, and pressing oils weren't going to give the natural hair enthusiast what they were looking for. The movement was as political as it was cultural and stylish.

Magnificent Products, a company from Los Angeles, filled this void for natural hairstylists. In the mid-1960s, **Dennis Taylor** and **Wilber Jackson** created products specifically for the afro hairstyle, then called the Natural. Magnificent Products shook up the Black haircare industry and their range made it tough for other brands, who were still in the mode of making products for pressing and straightening hair, to compete. J. Strickland & Co. also realized this, so they bought Magnificent Products. But the deal was a bad one; instead of incorporating the company, J. Strickland shut the company down after its acquisition. To quote that popular Connect Four ad from the early eighties, "Pretty sneaky, sis."

However, J. Strickland & Co. couldn't keep their monopoly over the Black hair market forever. Nowadays, Blue Magic has to compete with a plethora of natural hair care companies. These companies use much more sophisticated base ingredients and are more mindful of the different hair textures that exist within the Black American diaspora. This ran counter to how the old-school companies viewed Black hair products, which were all created to straighten or stretch out hair, regardless of density and texture. Gone are the days when Black Americans felt the only way they could be taken seriously by White America was by adhering to White beauty standards. Nowadays, there are a myriad of ways to express

Blackness naturally, and there are tons of products on the market that allow people to discover their individual style. Some of those companies include Shea Moisture, Mixed Chicks, and one of the biggest names out there, Carol's Daughter.

Carol's Daughter got its start in 1993 thanks to **Lisa Price**, who began developing hair care products in her Brooklyn kitchen after encouragement from her mother Carol, hence the name. She began selling her products at local flea markets and, in 1999, her popularity had grown to where she could open her own boutique in Brooklyn. Her business grew to have an online presence in 2000 and, in 2002, Price got the Oprah boost by being featured on *The Oprah Winfrey Show*.

As an established brand, Carol's Daughter launched on HSN, introducing Price to even more haircare lovers. Between 2014 and 2015, her growing line of products for hair, skin, and body were brought to Target and, within that same time span, Price's company was acquired by L'Oreal, firmly cementing her as a centerpiece in the natural haircare community. Carol's Daughter is now in thirty thousand retail locations around the US and, in 2017, Price was honored by having her company featured in the Smithsonian National Museum of African American History and Culture.

During the acquisition, fans noticed that the brand's marketing skewed a little toward all women with curly hair textures, or otherwise underserved hair textures, rather than just the ranges of African American hair. Some people took umbrage to this. But, at the end of the day, it can't be denied that Carol's Daughter revolutionized the hair industry with her focus on ethnic hair textures.

Richelieu Dennis, who we already met when learning about the new Madam C.J. Walker hair line, had his original claim to fame with his line of haircare products, Shea Moisture. He and **Nyema Tubman**, a direct descendant of abolitionist Harriet Tubman, started their company, Sundial Brands, as a way to make it in America. Hailing from Liberia, Dennis was able to escape his country's civil war by attending Babson College on scholarship. After his mother came to visit him for his graduation, their family home was destroyed by rebels. With no home to go back to, Richelieu made it his mission to become successful in America. He utilized his family's knowledge of hair, skin, and body products from recipes developed by his grandmother Sofi Tucker. He, his mother, and his sister named the company Shea Moisture and began selling their products in Harlem in 1992. Shea Moisture quickly became popular and street vendors began asking for products to sell. As the business grew, he and Tubman created Sundial Brands, which eventually became acquired by Unilever.

Sundial Brands, which also includes the Nubian Heritage line of products, is now a company worth one billion dollars, but thankfully, Richelieu also pays his fortune forward by creating the New Voices Fund, which is a hundred million dollar fund for women of color entrepreneurs that provides them with the tools to level the playing field and help them succeed. Incredibly, Richelieu is also now the owner of *Essence* magazine, which means the historic magazine will be able to continue influencing Black Americans for years to come.

While most natural hair brands on the market specifically market toward Black Americans that present as or identify as monoracial, there wasn't a brand out there that catered to the hair needs of biracial or multiracial Black Americans. Enter Mixed Chicks, created by friends **Wendi Levy** and **Kim Etheredge**, who created their line out of their garage in 2003. The range targets people with curly hair regardless of racial or ethnic makeup. The line also allows curly-haired multicultural people to buy one product instead of embarking on their usual journey of blending products to help their hair, leaving their hair bogged down under too much product.

Black Makeup Emerges

The makeup industry has come a long way in a short time regarding choices for darker complexions. Thankfully, younger generations won't ever have to know the struggle of being unable to find your shade or finding ashy shades that were supposed to be matches for your skin.

The company that put a dent in that scarcity was Fashion Fair Cosmetics. **Eunice W. Johnson**, the wife of *Ebony* and *Jet* owner John H. Johnson, was the creator of the brand in 1973, finding holes in the makeup market for women of darker complexions.

Johnson got the idea for the company when she noticed models hired for the Ebony Fashion Fair Show had to mix available tones together to get their proper shade. After finding that existing cosmetic companies were unwilling to create shades for Black women, she and her husband decided to hire a private lab to create foundation formulas based on the mixes the models had created themselves. After the models wore these new shades on the catwalk, the Johnsons debuted a capsule collection of makeup as a mail-order package in 1969. The line was an instant success, and Fashion Fair Cosmetics was born four years later as a brand aimed toward affluent department stores.

Fashion Fair's success also paved the way for other brands to come along in the 1990s, such as IMAN Cosmetics, created by world-famous supermodel **Iman**, in 1994. Like Fashion Fair, Iman created IMAN Cosmetics to cater to the underserved Black woman, but her line also extended itself to Asian, Latina, and multicultural skin tones. Rapper and actress **Queen Latifah** also got in the beauty game when she released her line of makeup, the Queen Collection, with CoverGirl in the early 2000s after she became a CoverGirl ambassador.

Queen Latifah said that she felt compelled to create her line after a fan approached her at the airport to congratulate her on her ambassadorship but complained how CoverGirl still didn't have her shade. Combined with Latifah's own experience with poor, ashy shade ranges throughout her life, she approached CoverGirl about strengthening their line.

The Queen Collection eventually became even broader, offering shades for all ethnic hues. Now CoverGirl has taken the Queen Collection idea and incorporated it into their brand proper, now offering a wider range of foundation shades.

Nowadays, there are even more brands to choose from that cater to Black skin tones. The biggest one out there right now is Fenty Beauty, owned by international singing superstar **Rihanna**.

I'd say that Rihanna's Fenty Beauty is like the Fashion Fair of the twenty-first century, since she, like the Johnsons, put the makeup world on notice by introducing a whopping forty foundation shades with her first line. Even though there was more visibility for darker shades in makeup before Fenty, cosmetic companies were dragging their heels when it came to providing proper mid-tones for Black Americans, whose skin tones run the gamut from super light to super dark. Even better is that recently she's debuted even more shades.

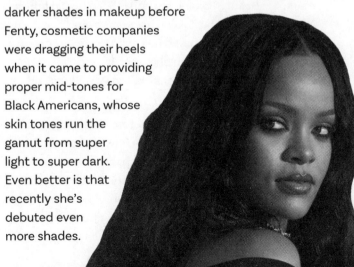

Mented Cosmetics founders **KJ Miller** and **Amanda Johnson** became the fifteenth and sixteenth Black women to raise a million dollars in seed capital for the business. Turns out they were only trying to raise $500,000 but doubled that goal, adding to Black women's entrepreneurial history.

Mented Cosmetics continues the explosion of Black-centric makeup with lipstick ranges specifically catering to Black women and other women of color looking for that perfect nude, a quest made difficult by how few brands will put out nude shades that actually match dark skin tones. Now, Mented includes a wide range of foundation for darker shades as well as a set of nude nail polishes that, like everything else Mented offers, caters to darker tones. They have also begun expanding into eyeshadow, making them a one-stop shop for women who are looking for products that are "their skin, but better."

One of the most ingenious Black-owned brands on the market is Beauty Bakerie started in 2011 by **Cashmere Nicole**. The brand has blown up so fast—and in such a short time—that the brand has even been shouted out by the likes of Beyoncé, along with *Essence, Teen Vogue, Allure, Forbes, InStyle, The Huffington Post, BuzzFeed* and many others.

Nicole was trained as a nurse before launching into the beauty business, but she always had an entrepreneurial spirit, even as a child. In her adult life, she acquired the life skills necessary to start Beauty Bakerie. Some of those are the result of her becoming a single teenage mother. Later, right before her makeup line came out, she was diagnosed with breast cancer, putting her line—and her life—at risk.

But throughout all of the ups and downs of her life, including a double mastectomy, she kept working on her beauty line, which earned a three-million-dollar investment from Unilever Ventures and is now a five million dollar business.

Her product line is based around the aesthetic of baking and sweetness, and that sweetness doesn't just stop at the pastel, dessert-themed packaging. Nicole's business has also allowed her to create Sugar Homes, which donates money, toys, clothes, and other essentials to orphanages around the world. The initiative's first project is with Uganda's female-led orphanage, The Hopeworth Children's Foundation. The initiative will help the foundation with the construction of their new orphanage and provide school fees, food, and clothes for the foundation's children.

The Lip Bar, a line of custom-made vegan lipsticks, started in 2012 and is another Black-owned brand that has risen from adversity toward astronomical success. I first saw The Lip Bar founder **Melissa Butler** on an episode of *Shark Tank*. At the time, she was trying to secure funding from at least one of the Sharks, investors who have made their fortunes in various sectors. As much as I was used to the Sharks ripping some inventors apart, I was taken aback by how much they let Butler have it just because she wanted to make uniquely colored lipstick.

Butler's goal was simply to create lipsticks without harsh chemicals in a line that features a wide range of cool and interesting colors. And that's what Butler has delivered. Now, her brand has grown to the point where it's sold in Target. So, it looks like the Sharks were wrong in their assessment of Butler's business. Who's had the last laugh now?

Pioneering Models

Today, a lot of people scoff at the modeling world, as if it's just a world of vapid people doing vapid things. But don't let the stereotypes fool you—this isn't *Zoolander*. The modeling world is full of people who are changing the nation's beauty standards, thereby changing views on race.

The models listed below not only broke the color barrier, but some also provided much-needed representation for LGBT Black Americans who also wanted to see themselves represented in a positive, beautiful way.

Donyale Luna, born as Peggy Ann Freeman, is credited as "the first Black supermodel," officially breaking the beauty standard mold. Of course, Black models were featured regularly in magazines like *Essence*, *Ebony*, and *Jet*. But Luna was the first to cross over into White mainstream publications, appearing in the April 1965 issue of *Harper's Bazaar* as the first Black woman to be featured on the cover. She then signed an exclusive year-long contract with the magazine's fashion photographer Richard Avedon.

She continued breaking barriers, becoming the first African American model on the cover of British *Vogue*, and her visage and figure were used as the inspiration for the first Black mannequin made in 1967. She also became a muse for famous surrealist painter Salvador Dali and earned the nickname "the reincarnation of Nefertiti."

A fun note for me, a journalist by trade: before her journey in fashion, Luna studied journalism at Cass Technical High School in her native Detroit. She also sang in the choir, showing that she was more than just a pretty face.

Even though Luna is believed to be the first Black supermodel in America, there's a bit of discrepancy as to whether she or **Naomi Ruth Sims** was truly first. If we go by the dates, Sims's first cover was for the October 17, 1969, issue of *Life*, breaking the color barrier for the magazine. However, as we see above, Luna's first cover was four years prior.

Maybe the discrepancy is the result of Sims starting to work on the runways in the late 1960s. She got her break with former Dutch model Wilhelmina Cooper, the founder of the now-infamous agency Wilhelmina Models. With Cooper's representation, Sims was featured on an AT&T national television campaign in designer clothes by American powerhouse Bill Blass. By 1970, she was one of the world's biggest names in the fashion industry. By 1973, Sims retired from modeling at twenty-five to start her own business, a multimillion-dollar wig and beauty company. She's also written five books on the industry and an advice column for young Black girls in *Right On!* magazine.

Luna and Sims's careers paved the way for **Beverly Johnson**, who launched her career with *Glamour* magazine in 1971; Johnson became the first African American model on the cover of American *Vogue* in 1974. Before her modeling career, she was an Olympic-qualifying competitive swimmer and went to Northeastern University in Boston on a full scholarship to study criminal justice. Even though she put her law school dreams aside for modeling, she managed to change the world with her presence by refashioning what it meant to be thought of as "the girl next door," a trope usually associated with White girls (think Betty Cooper from *Archie Comics*). Girls next door are generally thought of as "good" girls who are wholesome, innocent, and someone you'd like to bring home to your parents. On the flip side, Black girls were often hypersexualized even before reaching adulthood. They were also villainized, exoticized, and objectified. However, Johnson's athletic frame and beautiful looks earned her the moniker the "supergirl next door," changing the game for how Black beauty could be conceptualized.

Tracey Norman, also known as "Africa," broke more than just the color barrier. She is America's first Black transgender model (appearing on a Clairol hair color box in the 1970s), the second African American woman to be featured on the cover of *Vogue*, and one of the first openly transgender models on the cover of

Harper's Bazaar along with transgender model Geena Rocero in 2016. Throughout her career, she has been featured in *Essence* and has modeled for Avon as well as the aforementioned Clairol.

Norman endured hardship growing up, enduring sexual abuse from a neighbor as a child and struggling with her gender identity. Her mother accepted her for who she was. Norman had to make her name as a successful model before her father, who was then battling cancer, came to accept her without prejudice.

These trailblazers have made the way for models like **Leyna Bloom**. She is a biracial transgender model of Filipina and African American descent. Talented in various modes of dance, she originally went to Chicago Academy of the Arts with a full scholarship. However, she later dropped out after her scholarship wouldn't allow her to continue dancing at the school after her transition. She moved to New York and was homeless while working at a restaurant and performing in New York's underground ballroom scene. Her career in modeling exploded in 2017 when she became the first transgender woman to appear on the cover of *Vogue India*. Her career became even more viral when she launched her campaign to become the first transgender model to walk on the Victoria's Secret Fashion Show runway.

Beauty Is a Civil Right

As we learned earlier when reviewing the civil rights movement, there was an overabundance of men in powerful roles, while women were either pushed aside or desexualized as mothers of the movement instead of being represented as the activists they actually were. Many Black women were able to carve out a path for themselves and excel in the beauty and fashion world—a world that is, perhaps condescendingly, typically thought of as a woman's domain.

However, as we know, the world of beauty and fashion is far from "women's work." These industries are socially relevant and socially charged. They represent how we see ourselves, and, unfortunately, the industries are also used by the White supremacist systems to compartmentalize beauty by race and culture. Regardless of the deck that's stacked against them, Black women have succeeded by breaking boundaries, reinventing the standards, and creating brand new beauty and fashion moments pop culture historians will be talking about for decades to come.

Chapter 6

Black American Environmentalists

The environment is a hot topic these days, both literally and figuratively. But hardly anyone ever talks about what is actually being done to help save the planet and at-risk habitats. Most of the press's energy regarding climate change seems geared toward scary statistics and predictions instead of the people who are putting boots to the ground, saving the planet and making sure those predictions don't come true. The solutions are clearly there, and many scientists and activists are doing their best to implement said solutions to make life better, not only for their families, but for people around the planet who are facing the brunt of climate change. A lot of those boots on the ground belong to Black environmentalists and activists who are doing the hard work of protecting the environment but rarely getting the credit, since the environmental discussion is most often skewed toward White influencers and organizations.

More importantly, those getting the most attention not only have more capital to work with, but they are usually working from a place of privilege. It's not their neighborhoods that are being used as the building ground for plants that pollute the groundwater and the air alike. They aren't the ones living next to landfills or other undesirable locations that White neighborhoods are far from. In short, they aren't usually the victims of ecoracism, the practice of using negative environmental factors to harm people of color or low-income families.

The Foundations of Black Environmentalism

The term "environmental racism" (or "ecoracism") has been around since its development in the 1970s and 1980s. **Benjamin Chavis**, the former executive director of the United Church of Christ Commission for Racial Justice, defined environmental racism as "racial discrimination in environmental policy making, the enforcement of regulations and laws, the deliberate targeting of communities of color for toxic waste facilities, the official sanctioning of the life-threatening presence of poisons and pollutants in our communities, and the history of excluding people of color from leadership of the ecology movements."

The person we can thank for expanding on the study of ecoracism and bringing ecoracism discussions to the forefront of modern environmentalism is **Robert Bullard**, who is considered the father of environmental justice. It's surprising that we haven't heard a lot in the media about Bullard's hallowed place in environmentalism, especially since his work revolves around the people who could be the most impacted. His groundbreaking work on environmental racism started with his 1994 paper, "The Legacy of American Apartheid and Environmental Racism," in which he defined environmental racism as a practice that "refers to any policy, practice, or directive that differentially affects or disadvantages (whether intended or unintended) individuals, groups or communities based on race or color."

Bullard's accolades include being named as one of TheGrio's 100 Black History Makers in the Making in 2010, receiving the 2017 Child Health Advocate Award from the Children Environmental Health Network, being called one of twenty-two Climate Trailblazers by the Global Climate Action Summit in 2018 and being named one of the world's 100 Most Influential People in Climate Policy by Apolitical in 2019.

Bullard was the founding director of Clark Atlanta University's Environmental Justice Resource Center before joining Texas Southern University as the dean of the Barbara Jordan-Mickey Leland School of Public Affairs, a position he held between 2011 to 2016. Bullard currently works as a distinguished professor of urban planning and environmental policy at TSU. In 2011, he also cofounded the HBCU Climate Change Consortium with **Dr. Beverly Wright**, the executive director of the Deep South Center for Environmental Justice. The Consortium is running to this day, its seventh HBCU Climate Change Conference took place in November 2019. The Consortium was created to "help raise awareness about the disproportionate impact of climate change on marginalized communities to develop HBCU students, leaders, scientists, and advocates on issues related to environmental and climate justice policies, community resilience, adaptation, and other major climate change topics—especially in vulnerable communities in the Southern United States where the vast majority of HBCUs are located and where more billion-dollar disasters occur than the rest of the country combined."

Bullard has published eighteen books and his focus over the course of his work revolves around the interconnectedness of problems such as environmental racism, industrial facility sitting, climate disaster, and emergency response with sustainable development, urban land use, community reinvestment, proper housing and transportation, and a community's ability to utilize smart growth and regional equity for community resilience and climate justice.

Wright, Bullard's partner with the HBCU Climate Change Consortium, is herself an environmental justice scholar and advocate as well as a civic leader and sociology professor. She is the founder and executive director of the Deep South Center for Environmental Justice, which addresses the unique health and environmental inequities facing people and habitats along the Louisiana Mississippi River Chemical Corridor and the Gulf Coast Region. The Center is a community-university partnership organization that gives education, safety and health training, and job placement to people living in communities impacted by climate change and environmental justice issues. Her work has allowed her to create a curriculum to teach young children in elementary schools, and this curriculum has been utilized by the New Orleans Public Schools, giving children a much-needed background in environmental justice. Wright also manages hazardous waste worker training programs that educate young people who live near Superfund and Brownfield sites for employment.

Warren Washington is the man who has helped us understand climate change to begin with. Washington is a rock star in the meteorology community as the current director of the Climate and Global Dynamics Division of the National Center for Atmospheric Research (NCAR) in Boulder, Colorado. Washington started with NCAR in 1963. His historic career revolves around his codevelopment of computer models that help scientists understand how climate change is impacting us today. Throughout his research, he has refurbished his models to include data about oceans and sea ice, giving scientists more information about what's going on in the environment.

As an expert on the subject of climate, Washington has advised several US presidents and Congress on climate issues and served on the President's National Advisory Committee on Oceans and Atmosphere from 1978 to 1984. Three years later, he was appointed to be NCAR director and, in 1994, he was elected as the President of the American Meteorological Society. He is also a fellow at the African Scientific Institute as well as the American Association for the Advancement of Science. He has written over a hundred professional articles on atmospheric science and the 1986 book he coauthored with Claire Parkinson, *An Introduction to Three-Dimensional Climate Modeling*, has become the gold standard scientists refer back to. Washington is the main reason we know so much about climate change, yet his name goes virtually unmentioned or unrecognized in the mainstream media.

One person who provided groundwork for modern Black environmentalism is someone we met in a previous chapter, **Fannie Lou Hamer.** While Hamer is mostly aligned with civil rights work, she is also part of the environmentalist movement for Black Americans in terms of fighting ecoracism. As we can tell from Hamer's overlapping interests and the overlapping interests of many in this chapter, racism and environmentalism do, in fact, go hand in hand. We usually think of the two areas of interest as being in silos differentiated from each other.

Hamer, as we learned, started the Freedom Farm Cooperative, which gave Black people the ability to own and farm collectively. Through star-studded support as well as a ten thousand dollar donation from Wisconsin-based organization Measure for Measure, Hamer started out with forty acres of land to allow poor sharecroppers and farmers the ability to chart their own financial course in their lives, free from the economic shackles of White landowners.

Farmers could join the co-op for just a dollar a month, which today seems absolutely unbelievable. Everyone should have been able to afford that, right? Wrong. We can't under-estimate how hardcore the economic disparity was for poor Black people, since only thirty families could afford to join even at just a dollar a month while 1,500 families were part of the co-op in name only.

However, the co-op grew over time and, by 1970, Hamer was able to purchase 640 acres to add to her co-op and, through the help of organizations like the National Council of Negro Women, she was able to create a piggy bank that provided food to poor families.

What's unfortunate is that the Freedom Farm co-op wasn't able to keep this growth going and, by the mid-1970s, it folded. To double the bad news, Hamer died a few years later in 1977. But we shouldn't think of her efforts a failure; her work regarding low-income housing, entrepreneurship, economic equity and land ownership are the cornerstones many of today's Black and POC-centered co-ops are based on. She is rarely given her moment in history, but she is one of the pioneers of the modern wave of Black ecoracism activists. Her work has influenced and will keep influencing those who want to create a society that is devoid of White supremacy and a centralized economy.

Now that we have a bit of a background on Black America's influence in environmentalism, let's talk about some of the movers and shakers in the contemporary Black environmentalism space.

Environmental Game-Changers

In the field of Black environmentalism, there is a lot of focus on problems that are happening *right now* as opposed to problems that could happen in the future. In order to prevent a dire future, it makes a lot of sense to stop what's happening in the dire *present*. Because let's face it—there's a lot of horrific stuff going on as you're reading this book, and many of these issues are affecting people of color, including Black Americans, the most.

The issues are varied and far-reaching, such as food deserts in neighborhoods and lack of access to clean water, like in Flint, Michigan, and in other pockets around the country. There are neighborhoods situated right next to plants or landfills or other industrial zones.

But there are people out there working to create a more equitable and sustainable future. Color me excited to learn that many of those people are Black American activists.

Rue Mapp, for instance, is the founder and CEO of Outdoor Afro, a national nonprofit organization that reconnects Black Americans to nature. Many Black Americans have a traumatized relationship with nature because of our collective history regarding slavery. Many in our families associate the outdoors with work, inequality, and injustice. My late maternal grandmother, for instance, loved seeing my dad's bountiful garden whenever she visited but hated gardening herself because of her childhood as a sharecropper, picking cotton in what is now known as Alabama's Black Belt. Because of her hard childhood, she never wanted to do anything remotely resembling picking again.

However, Black Americans also have a collective history of being connected to nature, thanks to those same enslaved ancestors who often did their best to keep their traditions from the African motherland alive. Outdoor Afro helps Black Americans reconnect with the outdoors and their roots. Through its work, the organization is changing ideas about conservation. Outdoor Afro makes conservation a communal experience by leading outdoor recreation activities such as biking, camping, and hiking. The nonprofit also educates about the environment and conservation stewardship, reaching thirty thousand people a year through the organization's physical events. Thanks to the advent of the internet, the organization has an audience of millions who know about the group and interact with its initiatives.

Mapp's work has helped the everyday person in a one-on-one setting, but she has also been able to leverage her work into a position in politics, by being invited to participate in the Obama administration's America's Great Outdoors Conference and First Lady Michelle Obama's "Let's Move" initiative. From 2010 to 2012, she also oversaw the Stewardship Council Foundation for Youth Investment's grant-making program.

Shelton Johnson would love what Outdoor Afro is doing. Johnson is a National Park ranger who grew up in the city of Detroit. However, he always had a love for the outdoors and became a seasonal worker at Yellowstone while working on his MFA in writing at the University of Michigan. What started as a way to have a peaceful place to write turned into a lifelong career; he worked not only at Yellowstone, but at the Great Basin and as an interpreter at Fort Dupont Park. In his work throughout the country, he has been able to influence other kids who, like him, grew up in the inner city with limited or no access to the great outdoors. He made it his mission to get these inner city kids interested in nature, and through serendipity, he came across the history of the Buffalo Soldiers: African American soldiers who patrolled the American West. Their main goal was to protect settlers, wagon trains, stagecoaches and railroad crews while keeping Native American tribes at bay.

Of course, there's a complicated history embedded in the fact that a group of people who were descended from slaves were fighting sanctioned battles against indigenous people embattled by the same foe—White supremacy. Despite this, the buffalo soldiers are a part of African American history, and as such, it gave Johnson a way to get Black kids to realize that they, too, have a place in the wonders of nature.

Johnson has told the tale of the Buffalo Soldiers since 1998. His time as a historian has provided him with opportunities to speak to children across America and educate groups with his fictional Buffalo Soldier character Sergant Elizy Boman.

While there are several organizations that aim to help Black Americans within the country's borders, there are also other organizations that aim to help native Africans on the continent since they, like us over here, are subject to the brunt of climate change.

The Sierra Leone Foundation for New Democracy, for instance, is one of those organizations leading the charge of protecting African nations from climate change's potential impact. **Sam Grant** is the cochair of the Board of Directors of the organization, which works with communities to build a foundation for people to utilize new, sustainable alternatives that "nurture democratic relationships and decision making among and across individuals, families, institutions, and the environment."

To quote the organization itself, its work is intent on "actively transforming extractive and exploitative dynamics by reviving Africa's nonviolent, deliberative traditions of decision making—the foundation for a new democracy—through the vehicles of Food Sovereignty & Ecological Resilience, Mass Critical Literacy, and Cooperative Economics." In short, the group is working on making Africa a place that harkens back to its philosophical and social roots to create a new, more sustainable way of life.

Grant's influence in the organization stems from his own background in Jacksonville, Florida, where he became affected by the area's racism at just seven years old when his family integrated a White neighborhood. As a social entrepreneur and a faculty member at Metropolitan State University in Denver, Colorado, Grant has worked since 1983 to create solutions for some of the most pressing environmental and economic issues of the day.

The Sierra Leone Foundation for New Democracy isn't the only organization Grant has founded. Some of his organizations include AfroEco, Organizing Apprenticeship Project, Full Circle Community Institute, The Green Institute Eco-Industrial Park, The Wendell Phillips Community Development Federal

Credit Union and Grassroots Public Policy Institute, among others.

Savonala "Savi" Horne is the executive director of the Land Loss Prevention Project in Durham, North Carolina. Her nonprofit law firm is part of the North Carolina Association of Black Lawyers and provides legal representation of clients as well as outreach and community economic development to promote land perseveration, wealth, and rural ways of life. Horne has been doing this work for over thirty-three years and has helped rural communities who are facing disadvantages in their businesses, particularly Black farming communities. Some of the threats these farmers face include regular difficulties like debt, but there's also the big threat of gentrification, a type of predatory appropriation in which landowners, usually Black or POC, have their land bought out by richer, usually White, land developers. Horne's work helps farmers fight these threats and provides them with the tools to make their farms more technologically savvy, sustainable, and, of course, financially "in the black."

Tanya Fields also works in the arena of food justice and land preservation, basing her work as the founder and executive director of the Bronx-based Black Feminist Project on her own life as a woman who has experienced food insecurity: the lack of access to affordable and nutritious food. Fields was a single working mother of four in New York City facing the inequalities common to many underserved and impoverished families. She founded her organization in 2009 to serve women of color by creating women-led economic development opportunities. The Black Feminist Project focuses on urban farming and the eradication of the blight on low-income communities of food deserts—the lack of businesses that make high quality fresh food accessible. Two years after forming her organization, it was nominated for a Union Square Award in 2011.

Some of Fields's work within The Black Feminist Project includes attempts at establishing an urban farm on underdeveloped land from the New York City Parks and within the South Bronx. She has created the 5,400 square foot Libertad Urban Farms and the South Bronx Mobile Market—a clean energy vehicle that is solar-powered and runs on vegetable oil—which distributes nutrition education along with nutritious food. Fields's organization also hosts the SBMM Buying Club, which supports local rural farmers and gives families access to locally grown food, as well as the Not Just Talk Summits, which allow women and young people the chance to showcase their work and narratives revolving around equality and justice.

Peggy Shepard is the cofounder and executive director of WE ACT for Environmental Justice, also located in New York City. Whereas Fields primarily works in the Bronx, Shepard's work centers around upper Manhattan, engaging residents in the importance of environmental protection and health. She focuses primarily on environmental policy and environmental justice in urban communities and works to provide low-income residents clean, healthy neighborhoods.

The organization got its start in 1988 when Shepard and two other communities leaders reacted to the ecoracism that was taking place in their neighborhood in West Harlem. The community-based organization is now influencing policy in both New York and Washington DC. It continues to engage new generations of environmental activists through their People of Color Environmental Leadership Summits in DC and by acting as the lead organizer of the Environmental Justice Leadership Forum on Climate Change, which affects environmental policy in New York and the Northeastern United States. The group has been able to get several acts passed that have helped New York and the Northeast live healthier, more environmentally friendly lives.

Ron Finley is one of my personal favorites, since he does what my dad does in his backyard: aggressive gardening. I've grown up with gardens in our family yard, thanks to my father's obsessive love for gardening, so I feel like he and Finley would get along swimmingly.

Finley calls himself the "Gangsta Gardener" for various reasons. The first, I believe, is because of his roots in South

Central Los Angeles. We think of South Central as the epicenter of West Coast gangster rap, but, for Finley, the community is, in his words, a "food prison." South Central is notorious not just for its musical prowess, but for its lack of access to fresh food in its Black and Brown neighborhoods. Finley grew up knowing what it feels like not to have fresh produce or produce grown without pesticides, so he started his Gangsta Gardener crusade in 2010, growing vegetables in a small patch of dirt next to his home. From those humble beginnings grew Finley's life of food justice activism.

Finley earned his gangster nickname because of those same strips of dirt Finley was utilizing for his produce. The more Finley grew, the more he was breaking the law; those seemingly innocuous strips of land were owned by the City of Los Angeles, and the strips, which are technically called "parkways," couldn't be utilized without a permit. This led Finley to take on the system. He started a petition with other activists, demanding that the city allow people the right to garden in the neighborhood. He was successful and, because of his efforts, the city now allows public gardens on those parkways. His fight against the system also brought him national attention, launching him into a new stratosphere of activism. His work now includes all manner of community revitalization revolving around urban gardening. His biggest project yet is planning an urban garden in South Central called "HQ" that will, like its name, be the community's headquarters for fresh fruits and vegetables.

Omar Freilla is another activist with his home base in New York City. His organization, Green Worker

Cooperatives, is based in the South Bronx and works with the borough's communities of color and immigrant communities to create and sustain worker-owned green businesses. Like his fellow NYC activists, his work is rooted in creating a stronger community-owned economy, which not only enriches the lives of the business owners, but also the neighborhood itself with a lifestyle that supports equity among genders and races.

As the creator of Green Worker Cooperatives, Freilla is credited as being the creator of the academy model of cooperative development based on his more than thirteen-year history within the green business and cooperative space. He's also spent a commiserate number of years fighting many issues that affect marginalized communities, including the enemy we're currently investigating in this chapter, ecoracism.

Jeaninne Kayembe and **Devon Bailey** cofounded the Philadelphia-based Urban Creators with Alex Epstein. Kayembe, a Black queer thought leader and multimedia artist, and Bailey, a community leader and mechanical jack of all trades, cofounded Urban Creators to revitalize the city's eyesore areas into beautiful gardens and urban farms. Their first project was to create a farm out of a two-acre garbage dump. But now, they have transformed over three acres of land in Philadelphia and have given five thousand students and volunteers opportunities to get closer to nature. Because the local population—including artists and other creators—has been supported by Urban Creators, there's been a positive effect throughout the community. The organization's work has contributed to a 40 percent decrease of Part I Violent crime (a description that includes crimes such as murder, homicide, burglary, rape, and other offenses) since 2008.

Kayembe and Bailey's personal stories are just as interesting as their organization's impact. Kayembe, for instance, cofounded Urban Creators when she was just nineteen years old. Since becoming the organization's co-executive director, Kayembe is also the executive producer of the HoodStock Community and Arts Festival, which gives the city government, local artists, and the area's underserved communities chances to collaborate. She is also the consultant for Youth Speaks, which helps literary organizations build their impact through community and civic engagement and sustainable programming.

While Kayembe came to Philadelphia from California, Bailey is a native of North Philadelphia, with his family roots deep in the area. His grandfather, for instance, became a business owner and property owner after moving to Philadelphia from the South, despite only having a fifth-grade education. Bailey's grandfather's talents seemed to have traveled to Bailey, who is also a property owner and developer. Additionally, he is fluent in carpentry, home remodeling, landscaping, plumbing, roofing and mechanics.

Like Kayembe, **Destiny Watford**, the cofounder of student organization group Free Your Voice, is another example of how anyone can positively impact the world, regardless of age. Watford was sixteen years old when she won the 2016 Goldman Prize for her environmentalism within her own community.

Watford grew up in Curtis Bay, an industrial community in Baltimore, Maryland, that is notorious for inviting new plants or refineries into its borders. While those plants might generate money and jobs, they also generate tons of pollution, which was affecting the health of its citizens. Case in point: a study found Baltimore to be the deadliest city for air pollution in 2013, with 130 out of every 100,000 residents likely to die from long-term exposure to air pollution.

Another source of air pollution, the country's largest trash incinerator, was about to be built in Curtis Bay by Energy Answers in 2010, with the strange promise of bringing "clean" energy to the state. Of course, you might be wondering, how could those claims even be possible when the incinerator was expected to burn four thousand tons of trash, and not just local trash, but garbage brought into the city from elsewhere? Clearly, those claims were false, since operations would lead to various health problems. To be clear, it was determined that burning that much trash could release more mercury than the worst coal-powered plants, and it would be located within a mile from two of the area's public schools. Watford went to one of those schools, and, when she learned of the plan for the incinerator, she gathered together local residents to fight against the incinerator being built.

She and her fellow students walked up and down the neighborhoods, canvassing for support and organizing protests and petitions. She and her student-activists also attended a school board meeting to demand that the school board—which had agreed to buy in energy from the incinerator—divest. That next year, the school board voted to terminate its contract with Energy Answers, and by that fall, all twenty-two customers who had signed on with the incinerator terminated their contracts as well. By 2016, the Maryland Department of the Environment declared the incinerator dead; the incinerator's permit was now invalid. Watford, Free Your Voice, and her Curtis Bay residents won after years of being subjected to waste and pollution.

For a town that had been steeped in the malaise of their health and social concerns going unanswered for the sake of profit, the incinerator battle renewed the hearts and minds of Curtis Bay residents and gave Watford and her group the fortitude to keep fighting for clean energy. Currently, the area wants the land that would have been used for the incinerator to be dedicated toward actual clean energy, such as a recycling center and community solar farm. None of this would have been possible if it wasn't for Watford's intense focus on being heard.

Kari Fulton also knows the journey of fighting for justice early in one's life. She is currently the interim director of the Environmental Justice and Climate Initiative (EJCC), but before, she was the organization's National Youth Campaign coordinator. She is actively shaping upcoming generations of climate activists through her work.

She has led the EJCC through its partnership with the Energy Action Coalition to create youth summits such as Power Shift 2009, which became the largest lobby day and youth summit on climate change in the nation's history. She also cofounded Checktheweather.

TV, which gives young environmental activists of color a place online to spread their stories and messages of environmental justice. Who knows? Through Fulton's work, we might already have the next Kayembe or Watford in our midst, ready to usher us into another way of life.

Dr. Rose Brewer falls in the same vein as a Fannie Lou Hamer as her activism is made up of several different disciplines. These include the study and discussion of Black feminism, the prison-industrial complex, environmental justice, and other related issues. She has said that her work in environmental justice is "deeply connected to an African-rooted value system" and she utilizes that system in her work as the chairperson of the board of Environmental Justice Advocates of Minnesota, a coalition of community leaders and activists who support sustainable, fair local economies that promote universal access to safe environments. She is currently a professor of Afro American and African studies at the University of Minnesota—Twin Cities.

Christopher Bradshaw is taking care of environmentalism in the Washington DC area. He's the founder and executive producer of Dreaming Out Loud, Inc., which works toward creating food equity for the area's underserved communities.

Bradshaw's vision for change led him from Howard University, where he was studying political science and business, to create Dreaming Out Loud, which addresses the staggering statistics surrounding DC's impoverished communities, which includes exorbitant numbers of residents living in food deserts and without a high school diploma. On top of that, there's a lack of jobs for these residents, leading to higher-than-normal unemployment rates. These issues compound to create a perfect storm of poor health, including higher rates of diabetes. To combat these issues, Dreaming Out Loud uses a multipronged approach of combining food hubs, farmers' markets, urban farming, and other direct-to-consumer methods to bring these residents the food they so desperately need to have a healthy life. The result is twofold: families are finally able to have access to healthy produce, and the unemployment rate is addressed by a focus on entrepreneurship.

Similar to Brewer's focus on African principles, Dreaming Out Loud also uses African culture to define its mission. Their Adinkra Core Values are comprised of West African symbolism to showcase their focus on community living and sustainability.

Bradshaw's work has also led him to become a member of the first DC Food Policy Council, furthering his goal to increase food equity among DC neighborhoods.

While food equity is one thing, sustainable housing is another. If we're going to live fully sustainable lives, we need housing and buildings to match, and that's where **Kimberly Lewis** comes in.

Lewis is the senior vice president of market transformation and development in North America for the US Green Building Council (USGBC) in Washington DC. Her personal and career focus is on creating housing equity for families of all income levels, leading her to become the White House Champion of Change for Clean Energy in 2011. Within that same year, she was also named the inaugural president of the Green Meetings Industry Council's Greater Washington Area Chapter. She has also founded the Greenbuild International Conference & Expo as well as the USGBC Women in Green leadership platform events. She is also the governance chair on the board of directors for DC area community solar and clean energy development organization Groundswell and the Green Building Foundation's former chair of the board of trustees.

Mark Davis is also knee-deep in the solar and clean energy arena. In fact, he's the founder of the Washington DC-based WDC Solar, the first African American owned solar manufacturing plant in the United States.

A former NBA player, Davis grew his love for the environment during his childhood in Georgia, where he was raised on a farm. His environmentalism led him to become interested in green energy, the foundation of his business. WDC Solar allows Davis to provide free solar energy to DC's low-income residents. His company has also created nearly twenty high-paying jobs. How's that for growing the alternative economy? Even better, you can apply for a job simply by having a GED, meaning that WDC Solar is also reducing the amount of career inequity DC residents face, especially those with just a high school education.

The company is also helping residents save money; with 30 to 35 percent of income saved on energy bills, Davis told CNN that his customers are able to put that money toward more useful things, such as medication, education, grocery bills, and more. Who would have guessed all of that could happen simply by switching to solar?

Apparently, the rich know, since up until WDC Solar, it was only the rich who could afford retrofitting their homes with solar panels. Thankfully, things have shifted in the years since the company was founded in 2009, but solar energy panels continue to be too costly for a low-income family, meaning living sustainably in that way is out of the question. The rich, Davis noted, were taking advantage of the tax system, which rewards people with credits for using renewable energy. This allowed them to pay off the then-exorbitant upfront fees of purchasing solar panels.

Most low-income families don't have the time to play around with money in this fashion. Davis finally saw his opportunity to give other families the ability to get into the solar world when President Obama encouraged solar and renewable energy production as part of his economic stimulus bill. Davis was able to use the government's investments and incentives to develop his company, along with the help of funding from the DC Sustainable Energy Utility and later from the Sustainable DC Fund. He also took solar panel installation classes himself since he couldn't find any qualified installers. From what he learned, he created a training guide for entry-level installers. He's now advanced his company by opening up a branch in New York. The company is also planning to expand to Baltimore and Atlanta.

WDC Solar has also offered solar energy help internationally; after the devasting 2010 earthquake in Haiti, WDC Solar worked with ARCH trainees to create portable "solar suitcases" that could generate power for the country's hospitals, orphanages, and other facilities.

Gilbert Campbell III and **Antonio Francis** are also solar entrepreneurs. As the cofounders and managing partners of their Washington DC-based company, Volt Energy, they have grown their company to become one of the largest minority-owned solar energy development firms in the country. They build and operate solar energy systems for businesses, schools and industrial endeavors, and at an affordable price.

Campbell and Francis's company has earned the respect of its peers through its work with the American Association of Blacks in Energy and the Center for Energy Research and Technology at North Carolina A&T. Also noteworthy is the company's work with the US Department of Energy's Minorities in Energy Initiative.

Felicia M. Davis also works within the green building industry as the director of the UNCF's Building Green Initiative at Clark Atlanta University. The initiative is within the Atlanta University Center, the largest consortium of HBCUs in America.

As the director of the Building Green Initiative, Davis is helping the program advance its efforts at sustainability and green building at colleges that cater to POC students, such as HBCUs, institutions that serve Hispanic students, and Native American tribal colleges. Her HBCU Green Fund, a project she is currently working on, will also help colleges that cater to marginalized communities reach their environmental goals.

If you're spiritual, then you've probably thought about the spiritual side to environmentalism as well. To paraphrase the Bible, man is supposed to be the steward of the earth. This has been misinterpreted over time as humans being able to do what they please to the earth. Instead, we should take this statement for what I believe it means, which is that man is supposed to take stock of the world and protect its environments by seeing the spirituality of God within all living things on earth.

Perhaps that idea is what led **Ibrahim Abdul-Matin** to combine his Islamic studies with his environmental activism. His book, *Green Deen: What Islam Teaches about Protecting the Planet*, was published in 2010. It gives examples of how the practices and scriptures of Islam intersect with environmentalism and the calling humans have to protect the earth.

Outside of being an author, Abdul-Matin has worked for years in the realms of sustainability, new media, community engagement, technology, and sports. He's worked with New York Mayor Bloomberg as sustainability policy advisor and currently works as the New York City Department of Environmental Protection as the director of community affairs. He has also helped found the Brooklyn Academy for Science and the Environment.

John Francis is another activist who sought a spiritual path through environmentalism, but his journey was much different than Abdul-Matin's. Francis started his journey in the 1970s, giving up using motorized vehicles after he saw how an oil spill in the San Francisco Bay affected the area. Later, he took a vow of silence that lasted a staggering seventeen years. During that vow, he walked across America by foot to raise awareness for world peace and the environment. Somehow, throughout all of that walking, he also earned a PhD in environmental studies and a figurative degree in the human condition. He listened to people and the environment itself, and it was through this trek that he was able to ascend to the level of policymaker.

In 1990, when he ended his vow of silence, he became a goodwill ambassador for the United Nations Environmental Program and contributed to the Oil Pollution Act of 1990, written up to impact transportation regulations after the Exxon Valdez oil spill. He also translated his own experience of walking through the environment in his nonprofit environmental education organization Planetwalk, and in his 2009 book *Planetwalker: 22 Years of Walking. 17 Years of Silence.* His musings on silence continued in his second book, 2011's *The Ragged Edge of Silence: Finding Peace in a Noisy World*, published by National Geographic.

Leading the Charge

From civil rights to energy equity to food justice, environmentalism is a lot more than just a hipster pastime. For many of these activists, environmentalism is a present-day, active practice. Hopefully, this chapter did more than just let you know about some cool individuals. I hope it showed you that Black Americans are not only contributing to the environmental conversation but are actively providing solutions to the issues we face.

We all need to do our part to usher in the new world alongside these activists. More than that, it requires everyone's *belief* that they can do better. Whether that's recycling your plastic and aluminum or going to a city council meeting to demand that they provide solar retrofits or close that oil company or oil mine, believe you can make that positive impact. All small efforts lead to bigger, greater change.

THE BOOK OF
Awesome
BLACK
AMERICANS

Chapter 7

Black STEM

The world of STEM is a broad and fascinating field of scientists, engineers, doctors, and inventors who help make the world a better place. Unfortunately, that field is often depicted as being largely White. When we think of a scientist, we don't typically think of a Black person.

That doesn't mean STEM hasn't been impacted by Black Americans. On the contrary, Black Americans have contributed greatly to the country's scientific advancements and continue to do so. In fact, we've already met a few such impactful people in previous chapters. Benjamin Banneker, for instance, was a whiz at astronomy and created a reliable farmer's almanac as well as the first clock built in America. Otis Boykin invented a device that would change heart health forever, the pacemaker. Marie Van Brittan Brown invented the home security camera. Lonnie Johnson utilized a career as a NASA engineer to create the Super Soaker. Lewis Latimer patented the carbon filament for the lightbulb. Warren Washington created the computer models that allow scientists to study the effects of climate change. And Frederick McKinley Jones reinvented refrigeration for trains and trucks, which revolutionized how we ship and buy produce from all sectors of the country. Even the beauty inventors, like Madam C.J. Walker, Marjorie Stewart

Joyner, Annie Turnbo Malone, and others participate in the STEM conversation by inventing products that either rely on chemical or electrical know-how.

But of course, there are many other Black STEM role models I haven't mentioned yet. For instance, there's the story of the great Hidden Figure herself, **Katherine Johnson**. Johnson's role within NASA helped create a viable path for other Black women who want to learn more about earth, the planets, and the universe.

Black Americans in Space

If you're a fan of entertainment, you probably already know the gist of Johnson's story as Taraji P. Henson portrayed her in the 2016 Academy-nominated film *Hidden Figures*, which recounts how Johnson's calculations sent John Glenn on the US's first successful space launch.

But there is more to Johnson's story aside from sending a man to the moon. Johnson's civil rights activism began even before she came to NASA. She was one of the three Black students chosen to integrate her graduate school in West Virginia. What she endured as one of the first integrated students in West Virginia's graduate schools opened the doors for other Black people after her. Indeed, like other students who were tasked with being civil rights figures (like our friend from Chapter 3, Ruby Bridges) her experience allowed later generations of Black Americans to attend schools that would give us proper education and better quality of life.

Johnson worked as a teacher in a Virginia Black public school until 1952, when a relative told her about the National Advisory Committee for Aeronautics (NACA) looking for workers for their all-Black West Area Computing division. The division was overseen by another Hidden Figure, **Dorothy Vaughan**.

Vaughan had come to NACA's Langley Memorial Aeronautical Laboratory in 1943 after working as a math teacher in Virginia. She became a part of the West Area Computing division, which was a vital part of NACA. Even though the committee was segregated—down to the use of assigned bathrooms— and despite clear discrimination, Vaughan became NACA's first Black supervisor and one of NACA's few women supervisors. Her position gave Vaughan access to the entire laboratory, and she corresponded with White computers (not the devices, but the humans doing mathematical computations) as well as the Black women who worked under her in her division. She became efficient in FORTRAN programming and contributed to the SCOUT (Solid Controlled Orbital Utility Test) Launch Vehicle Program, which is comprised of a four-stage fuel satellite system with the ability to launch a 385-pound satellite into a 500-mile orbit. She was a vital part of NACA and NASA before retiring in 1971.

What did Johnson do under the supervision of Vaughan? She worked in the Maneuver Loads Branch of the Flight Research Division and worked in the division for four years, analyzing data from flight tests and investigating a plane crash caused by wake turbulence.

Unfortunately, after she'd completed this work regarding flight tests, her husband died of cancer in 1956. While this might have been one of the lowest points in her life, one of the highest points was right around the corner. Johnson's mathematics were relayed in a series of lectures by Flight Research Division engineers regarding space travel. The lectures, called Notes on Space Technology, provided the background for NACA to create their Space Task Group, the first official step NACA took toward going to space. As NACA transitioned to NASA (National Aeronautics and Space Administration), Johnson began working on analysis for space missions, such as the May 1961 Freedom 7 mission, the country's first spaceflight by a human. She also became the first woman in the Flight Research Division to get an authorial credit on a research report, thanks to a paper she coauthored with engineer Ted Skopinski, "Determination of Azimuth Angle at Burnout for Placing a Satellite Over a Selected Earth Position."

The story from *Hidden Figures* begins in 1962, when Johnson was tasked with computing the trajectory of Glenn's Friendship 7 mission. Glenn personally requested Johnson's calculations because, at the time, the electronic computers were unreliable. According to Johnson's recollection, Glenn said, "If she says they're good, then I'm ready to go." He—as well as all of NASA—put all of his trust into her numbers. Johnson's computations were not only sound, but resulted in a successful launch and splashdown, marking America's advancement in the Space Race.

Johnson accomplished much more during her time with NASA before her retirement in 1986. She authored or coauthored twenty-six research reports, did calculations that helped synch Project Apollo's Lunar Lander with the Command and Service Module orbiting the moon, and contributed to the Earth Resources Satellite, which allows NASA to monitor the earth's oceans, ice caps, coastal areas, and atmospheric readings, among other calculations. If we want to make some connections, we can realize that this very satellite is what allows NASA to help scientists study climate change and provide recommendations to fight against it. Johnson's contributions to science cannot be underestimated.

The road Johnson paved allowed another great Black woman, **Mae Jemison**, to become the first Black female astronaut.

Growing up, Jemison was one of my personal heroes because, aside from being the first African American woman to go to space in 1992, she credited her interest in space to *Star Trek*. Most importantly, she cited **Nichelle Nichols**'s character Nyota Uhura as her inspiration. I was a big *Star Trek* fan as a kid, and I'm still a big Trekkie today, so that fact has always endeared her to me. Think of my surprise when I realized she's also an Alabamian! She was born in Decatur, Alabama, but moved to Chicago when she was three. While she probably considers Chicago her hometown, she's a native Alabamian to me, and I'm proud to share a state with her.

Uhura's influence on Jemison shows us how entertainment can blur the lines between "fantasy" and "inspiration." The famous story that many Trekkies know is that Dr. King himself convinced Nichols to stay on the show as Uhura, a role she was considering giving up. Not only was he a fan of the show, but he knew the importance her role would have on young Black girls. That vision was made a reality by Jemison and others who follow the stars with the Starfleet mission statement in their hearts.

Appropriately for the character, Nichols herself has a keen interest in space travel, so much so that she flew as a part of the C-141 Astronomy Observatory, which analyzes the atmospheres of Mars and Saturn. Even though Nichols, a former singer and dancer for Duke Ellington's band, originally had misgivings about her role, she became a vital part of *Star Trek* fandom, so much so that, during the late 1970s through the late 1980s, Nichols was part of NASA's recruitment initiatives. Her work with NASA compelled many POC recruits to join, including **Guion Bluford**, who became the first African American astronaut in 1983 (whereas Jemison was the first African American female astronaut). Her new recruits also included **Ronald McNair**, the second African American astronaut, who sadly died aboard the tragic Challenger launch in 1986.

Life-Changing Doctors

The doctor's office. We don't like going, but we have to. Same for the dentist, the eye doctor, and other medical specialists. But I bet you seldom realize that when you're stepping into your doctor's office, you're stepping into Black American history.

Granted, that knowledge probably won't make you want to run to your doctor with joy since America's early medical history includes abuse toward African American slaves. For instance, if you're a female like me, you probably have complex opinions about the dreaded pap smear. Those feelings are valid, since the tools and techniques developed for that practice, as well as other gynecology practices, were developed by James Marion Sims.

Sims might be considered the father of modern gynecology as well as someone who contributed to the history of modern medicine. But he came by his fame at the cost of human indignity. Sims did experiments on enslaved women under the theory that Black women didn't experience pain in the same way White women did. In fact, he believed that Black women didn't experience pain *at all.* That led to all sorts of violent invasions of privacy, which allowed for the creation of the speculum, that metal device that gets inserted into a female's genitals during a pap smear. To be fair, the speculum has been moderately updated with models being made in smooth plastic rather than metal to reduce pinching. But the overall design hasn't changed since its inception. Also, while there's been a movement to redesign the tool for pap smears, it's taking a while for any new design to become an everyday part of gynecological practice.

Clearly, Sims isn't a great African American—he was a White doctor, and a nefarious one at that. He's featured here because it's important that we know the extent to which White supremacy features in our everyday lives, even in your standard doctor's visit.

Sadly, the misuse of Black people's bodies doesn't end with the development of gynecology. There's also the **Tuskegee Study of Untreated Syphilis in the Negro Male**, otherwise known as simply the Tuskegee Experiment, which began in 1932 and lasted until 1972 in Macon County, Alabama. The US Public Health Service studied 600 men—399 with syphilis and a control group of 201 men without syphilis—to see how the disease affected the human body. Clearly, the forty-year experiment was highly unethical for various reasons, not only because the control group was being lied to. These men were told they were being treated for "bad blood," which could refer to a plethora of illnesses, but, instead, they were being infected with the disease.

The main reason the study could go on for so long is because America viewed African Americans as dispensable. That a country could perform experiments on its own people should be considered heinous. The study was only unearthed and revealed to the public after a San Francisco-based PHS venereal disease investigator, Peter Buxtun, leaked the news to a friend who happened to be a reporter. That friend then sent the story to Jean Heller of the Associated

Press, who brought the study to the mainstream consciousness in 1972. Not only did the government knowingly infect healthy Black men, but, by not informing those men of their status, they allowed them to pass the disease on to their spouses and children. This worsened these people's quality of life, already made poor thanks to racism, discrimination, and poverty.

And poor **Henrietta Lacks** is also one of the more modern examples of Black people's bodies being used without consent for the sake of science and medicine.

Lacks was a young wife and mother to five children. Her life was full of family, but, while her focus in life might have simply been being a good wife and mother, Lacks's cells have impacted the study of cancer research and treatment. After Lacks was diagnosed with cervical cancer in 1951, she received radium treatments at Johns Hopkins Hospital, one of the few hospitals to treat poor Blacks. Unfortunately, the treatments didn't help her survive the illness, and she died in October of that year at thirty-one years of age.

While she was at Johns Hopkins, hers were among many patients' cells retrieved by the hospital for research. Dr. George Gey, who studied the cells of the hospital's cervical cancer patients, noticed Lacks's cells were vastly different from those of other patients. While other cell samples died quickly, Lacks's cells doubled over twenty to twenty-four hours. The cells—referred to as "HeLa" cells, after Lacks—have been widely shared and used for research. They have led to major breakthroughs in medicine, and not just in cancer research: they've been used in the development of the polio vaccine, research on the effects of zero gravity, and research on viruses such as AIDS.

While Johns Hopkins never profited from Lacks's cells, unethical practices were taken to acquire them, as informed consent did not take place—Lacks didn't know her cells were being used for further research. There was also a lack of communication with research participants and tissue donors, and a lack of privacy when it comes to medical records. Today, the hospital includes a committee tasked with deciding who can use Lacks's cells. Thankfully, the committee includes two members from Lacks's family.

Sadly, Lacks's original diagnosis of a malignant epidermoid carcinoma of the cervix was actually a misdiagnosis. The mistake was noticed in 1970, and physicians realized that Lacks actually had an adenocarcinoma, which originates in the glands, not the from the skin's surface or organ and tract linings. However, the misdiagnosis was common at the time.

A lot of instances in the scientific and medical fields have created distrust between Black Americans and medical professionals. However, Black Americans have made strides within the medical profession. This is great for the broadening of American history and American medical history. Even more importantly, these gains help rewrite the narrative for Black Americans when it comes to the doctor's office. If someone can see themselves in an industry, they can feel kinship with it. Thankfully, we are seeing more doctors, dentists, and specialists who look like us and care for our health.

Who are the trailblazers who have made the doctor's office a less racist place? Let's start with two women who broke through glass ceilings for Black women health professionals and Black professionals overall. Let's be honest—America hasn't been kind to women, especially Black women. We've already covered some of the injustices Black women have experienced, including what the medical profession has done to them. Let's not forget, however, that plenty of Black women have proven the status quo wrong. Three more women to add to that list include **Rebecca Lee Crumpler, MD**, **Rebecca J. Cole, MD**, and **Helen Dickens, MD.**

Crumpler, for instance, became the first Black woman to gain a medical degree from an American university. As you'll read below, there is one famous doctor who went to Canada to gain a medical degree for fear of not being able to achieve his goals in the States. But Crumpler succeeded in 1864 after graduating from the New England Female Medical College in Boston. She accomplished this feat during a time that wasn't only hostile to Black Americans, but to women as a whole in higher learning.

Crumpler was introduced to healthcare in childhood. She lived with her aunt who provided care for the sick in Delaware. Crumpler excelled in school, attending the West-Newton English and Classical School in Massachusetts, an elite private school. Afterwards, she worked as a nurse in 1852. In 1860, she applied for medical school and was accepted, leading her to historic accomplishments. Crumpler was the school's only Black graduate in 1864. Two years later, she and her husband moved to Richmond, Virginia, after the Civil War to care for Black patients. In fact, she was one of several Black doctors who provided their services to care for freed slaves who had no access to proper care. In her own words, she "[had] access each day to a very large number of the indigent, and others of different classes, in a population of over thirty thousand colored." Later in her career, she wrote a book on medicine called *A Book of Medical Discourses in Two Parts,* which was published in 1883. This book stands as one of the first medical publications written by a Black American.

Cole became the second Black woman doctor in the country in 1867 when she graduated from the Woman's Medical College of Pennsylvania. She was taught by the college's first female dean, Ann Preston. Cole's own intelligence served her well through the college and for her medical thesis; she wrote a paper called "The Eye and Its Appendages." Along with Preston's tutelage, Cole was able to gain clinical experience at New York Infirmary for Women and Children, run by Elizabeth Blackwell, the first woman ever to earn a medical degree in America. Blackwell praised Cole's skill in her autobiography, writing that she worked "with tact and care" and that the results she received from her careful medical care "serve to show that the establishment of such a department would be a valuable addition to every hospital."

After her time at the infirmary, Cole practiced medicine for fifty years, which included a practice in South Carolina and Pennsylvania. She also opened a Women's Directory Center in 1873 to serve destitute women and children. She was later named the superintendent of a home founded by the Association for the Relief of Destitute Colored Women and Children in Washington DC. Echoing Blackwell's assessment, the association found that Cole had "all the qualities essential to such a position—ability, energy, experience, tact." On top of that, she was noted as having a "cheerful optimism" that helped her patients as well as those around her.

Many years later, in 1950, OBGYN Helen Dickens, MD, followed in the footsteps of Crumpler and Cole and became the first Black woman admitted to the American College of Surgeons. Incredibly, she, the daughter of a former slave, rose to the heights of breaking ground in a profession rife with racism. Not only is she the first Black woman admitted to the American College of Surgeons, but she also became the associate dean of the University of Pennsylvania's Office of Minority Affairs, and, during the first five years of her tenure, she increased the university's minority enrollment to sixty-four students from just three.

Part of Dickens's success doesn't just rest on her intelligence. I think she realized that her accomplishments benefited from the efforts of those who came before her. When she was applying for medical schools and hospitals, she was encouraged by the achievements of others, including one of her mentors, **Dr. Elizabeth Hill**, the first Black physician to graduate from the University of Illinois. Hill helped her register for medical school and, because of Hill's efforts, Dickens became the only Black woman to graduate with a medical degree from the University of Illinois in the class of 1934.

A lot of Dickens's later work centered around sexual health and teen pregnancy, leading her to complete a survey to help parents, schools, and health professionals with intervention strategies to lower teen pregnancy and the transmission of STIs. She has been awarded for her work in this area, including accolades from the American Cancer Society and the Girl Scouts of Greater Philadelphia.

Dickens's daughter, **Jayne Henderson Brown, MD**, also took up the medical call like her mother, proving once again that pioneers pave the way for others to follow.

Edith Irby Jones, MD, made history in the South as the first Black medical student to integrate Southern medical schools. This pioneer died in 2019, which, like several entries in this book, puts into perspective just how recent a lot of our Black history actually is.

Jones made history when she was admitted into the University of Arkansas for Medical Sciences in 1948. But that wasn't her only accomplishment in breaking racial barriers. In 1952, she also became the first Black woman resident at Houston's Baylor College of Medicine. She cofounded the Association of Black Cardiologists in 1974 and became the first woman president of the National Medical Association in 1985. She, like so many featured, was the daughter of poor parents; in her case, her father was a sharecropper and her mother worked in homes as a domestic. Her sister's death from typhoid fever sparked Jones's interest in the medical profession. She did her sister's memory proud; not only did she grow up to practice medicine, she also changed the lives of many future Black doctors in the process.

Alexander Augusta, MD, gives us another first—he was the first Black physician appointed to the position of hospital director.

Alexander was born in Virginia in 1825. He received his medical education from Trinity Medical College in Toronto, Canada, and became the head of the Toronto City Hospital. Alexander came back to the States after writing to President Abraham Lincoln offering to work as a doctor for the "colored regiments" in the Civil War. He became the first African American to be commissioned as a medical officer in the Union Army and served as the surgeon-in-charge at the Contraband Hospital in Washington DC. (Term of note: "contraband" was often the term used for freed and enslaved Black people, which is interesting, seeing how these Black Americans' ancestors were *stolen* from Africa in the first place.)

Sadly, Augusta's work within the military was sidelined by racism. Among his other work within the Civil War, he was also given the title of regimental surgeon for the 7th Infantry of the United States Colored Troops in Maryland. However, the White surgeons weren't too keen on having a Black doctor as their superior, and they wrote to Lincoln to protest having to report to a Black man. Lincoln reassigned him to a Black troop recruiting station. While that assignment was not dishonorable, it's important to note how Augusta's talent and skill were seen as secondary to the color of his skin. Should it matter who is saving lives?

Apparently if you're raised in a racist environment, it does.

Despite inspiring many African Americans through his prestige, Augusta faced racism among civilians as well. One time, dressed in his army uniform, he tried to hail a streetcar on a rainy day in Washington DC. He wanted to stay dry from the rain, so he went to the area where White passengers sat. He was informed that he'd have to stand in rain-soaked area designated for Black passengers. When he refused, like Claudette Colvin and Rosa Parks would many years later, he was forced off the streetcar and had to arrive to his meeting soaked through.

What the passengers didn't know was that Massachusetts Senator Charles Sumner heard about what happened to Augusta and demanded that Congress allow Black Americans the same railroad privileges as their White counterparts. A year later, Black and White Americans were able to use whatever seat they preferred in the nation's capital.

Augusta continued to make history after the war. In 1868, he became part of the faculty of Howard University's new medical department. This appointment made him America's first Black faculty member in a medical school. He also served as a staff member of Freedmen's Hospital until 1877, when he left to set up a private practice in Washington DC. He remained in practice until his death in 1890.

Patricia Bath, MD, died in 2019, but she leaves behind a legacy of Black American history. Bath became the first Black woman physician to be awarded a patent for her medical invention. Her invention works in the lives of many Americans who have suffered from cataracts. She came up with a device for cataract surgery called the laserphaco probe, as well as a new technique, appropriately called laserphaco. Even though the technology wasn't available for her invention at the time she developed the idea in 1981, her invention was able to be fully realized and patented five years later. Today, the same technology Bath was able to use to recover the sight of people who had been blind for over thirty years continues to help those who suffer from cataracts.

This isn't the first time Bath has rocked the ophthalmic world. Between the late 1960s and early 1970s, Bath came up with a new discipline called "community ophthalmology," which combines community medicine, public health, and clinical ophthalmology to provide help to underserved people.

Her community ophthalmology was developed after her time as an intern at Harlem Hospital and Columbia University between 1968 to 1970. She realized that half of the patients in Harlem were blind or visually impaired, whereas only a few of the patients at Columbia University were. This led her to create a retrospective epidemiological study. She found that indeed blindness in the Black community was double that among their White counterparts, and the disparity was because of lack of access to proper eye care. Bath's community ophthalmology program has helped thousands of people whose eyesight would have gone untreated otherwise. Through the help of her volunteers, she has also given children with eyesight issues much-needed glasses, which have helped them in school and in life. She also compelled Harlem Hospital's Eye Clinic to start ophthalmic services in 1968, something the clinic didn't do at the time. Harlem Hospital completed its first eye surgery for free because of her persuasion. Also due to her efforts, professors at Columbia also started operating on blind patients for free, and she volunteered her services as an assistant surgeon.

She continued to make history in 1974 as the first woman faculty member in UCLA's Jules Stein Eye Institute Department of Ophthalmology. She was treated with indignity, however; she refused an office that was placed, as she described, "in the basement next to the lab animals." Her refusal led to her getting an appropriate office. But an appropriate office isn't all she received during her time there. By 1983, she was the chair of the Drew-UCLA ophthalmology residency training program, becoming the first woman in the country to have that position. In 1977, after taking her research to Europe, she and three others founded the American Institute for the Prevention of Blindness and she served as the organization's director.

Robert Boyd, MD, became the first president of the National Medical Association in 1895. The National Medical Association, described as "the collective voice of African American physicians and the leading force for parity and justice in medicine and the elimination of disparities in health," began in 1895. I think you can figure out why the group had to come into existence. The American Medical Association didn't allow Black physicians to enter the organization. To combat the rampant racism, the NMA was founded to give Black health professionals their own stance in the medical community. The charter members included Boyd as well as **Daniel Hale Williams, MD**, **Daniel L. Martin, MD**, **Miles V. Lynk, MD**, and **H.R. Butler, MD.** The organization's first issue of the *Journal of the National Medical Association* was published in 1909 and edited by **Dr. Charles V. Roman.**

We should be thankful that the NMA paved the way for the AMA to revoke its stance on racism within the organization and invite Black health professionals to its ranks. **Lonnie Bristow, MD,** in fact, became the AMA's first Black physician to head the group as president.

Bristow attributes his interest in medicine to his mother, who was a nurse at Sydenham Hospital in Harlem, New York. He said to the *American Medical News* that seeing his mother and others, "several races and several ethnic cultures linked by the common goal of providing compassionate care to patients" led him to his journey in medicine.

He opened his private practice in internal medicine outside of San Francisco and became active in the area of organized medicine, working with several organizations on the state and national levels. He joined the AMA in 1978 as an alternate delegate and, in 1979, he upgraded his affiliation within the organization as a full delegate. In 1985, he began climbing up the ranks in the organization, becoming the first African American to serve on the AMA board of trustees. He later became the AMA's first Black American chair of the board in 1993. He was appointed as the AMA's president in 1995, cementing the AMA's new stance on being inclusive and diverse.

Bristow's time as AMA president changed the association forever. Not only was Bristow making history, but he was opening the doors to other Black leaders within the organization, such as **Patrice Harris, MD**, the first Black woman president of the AMA.

While acting as president, Harris also retains her private practice as a psychiatrist in Atlanta. She is also an adjunct professor in Emory University's Department of Psychiatry and Behavioral Sciences. On top of all of that, she is also an adjunct clinical assistant professor in psychiatry and behavioral services at Morehouse School of Medicine. It's admirable that she's wearing so many hats while serving as president, proving that Black women have much talent and skill to give to whatever industry they apply themselves to.

Harris has had the same Black Girl Magic throughout her career. She has served on the American Psychiatric Association Board of Trustees and was the past president of the Georgia Psychiatric Physicians Association. Harris has served in several founding roles before becoming the AMA's first Black woman president. She was the founding president of the Georgia Psychiatric Political Action Committee and served as the founding chair of the AMA Opioid Task Force, which was created in 2014. Before her role as head of the task force, she was part of the AMA Board of Trustees since 2011 and was chair of the AMA Council on Legislation and cochair of the Women Physicians Congress.

Alexa Irene Canady, MD, is another first we must honor. In 1981, Canady became the first Black woman in the country to become a neurosurgeon.

Incredibly, Canady almost dropped out of college when she was in undergrad majoring in mathematics. She said that what made things better for her was when she learned of a chance to win a minority scholarship in medicine. Canady eventually earned her BS degree in zoology from the University of Michigan in 1971 and graduated from the university's medical school in 1975 cum laude. She has worked for twenty years in the area of pediatric neurosurgery, and, throughout that time, she has had to face racism and sexism. But her work spoke for itself, and during her tenure at the Children's Hospital of Philadelphia between 1981 and 1982, her coworkers voted her as one of the hospital's top residents. Her stellar record continued during her tenure as chief of neurosurgery at the Children's Hospital of Michigan from 1987 until her retirement in 2001. She has been honored by several organizations, including the Michigan Woman's Hall of Fame, the American Medical Women's Association, and the Wayne State University Medical School.

New Jersey native **Donna Marie Christensen, MD**, became the first physician elected to US Congress. Christensen, whose father is from the Virgin Islands, carried her medical practice into her federal advocacy in Congress. As the first female representative of the US Virgin Islands, she focused on improving the lives of her constituents. Some of the things she fought for included advocating for more economic opportunities and better living conditions. For her, the fight for living and economic conditions intersects with her constituents' medical care. "In my practice, you always find that there are a lot of social and other issues that impact the impact the health of your patients," she is quoted as saying. "Many times, people would come in just to talk about whatever problems they were having, so I kind of looked at it as bringing my office work from a local level to a larger, national level."

M. Joycelyn Elders, MD, became the first African American and the second woman to lead the US Public Health Service as Surgeon General in 1993. But her status as a historic Surgeon General isn't the only accolade Elders has to her name. In 1978, she was the first person in Arkansas to become board certified in pediatric endocrinology.

Elders was born in 1933 in an impoverished, segregated part of Arkansas. As the oldest of eight children to sharecropper parents, she worked with her siblings in the cotton fields and attended a segregated school thirteen miles from home. Elders attended Little Rock's Black liberal arts college, Philander Smith College. Even though she had a scholarship, she scrubbed floors for her tuition and she and her siblings completed chores for neighbors and picked extra cotton to pay for Elders's bus fare.

Elders initially only aspired to become a lab technician, but she became inspired by Edith Irby Jones. Jones spoke at a college sorority and after seeing Jones, Elders realized she could become a doctor too. She had never met a doctor until she was sixteen years old, but thanks to Jones, Elders realized the sky is the limit.

Throughout her education and career, which included joining the army and training in physical therapy at the Brooke Army Medical Center at Fort Sam Houston, Texas, Elders faced racism. For instance, when she was discharged in 1956 and enrolled at the University of Arkansas Medical School, she was required to use a separate dining room with the cleaning staff despite the *Brown v. Board* ruling.

Despite all of the racism rigamarole, Elders became the chief resident of the University of Arkansas. This meant she was in charge of all of the residents, which were comprised of only White men. This was the start of her ascent. In 1971, she became the university's assistant professor of pediatrics and, in 1976, she became a full professor. In 1967, she earned her degree in biochemistry.

Over her career, Elders has published over a hundred papers on pediatric endocrinology, particularly in the realm of growth issues and juvenile diabetes. She also studied sexual behavior, finding that young women with diabetes faced health risks if they became pregnant at a young age. Some of the health risks include spontaneous abortion or the possibility of an infant with congenital abnormalities. With her work, she helped patients keep track of their fertility and determine when the best time was to start a family.

Then-Governor Bill Clinton appointed Elders as the head of the Arkansas Department of Health in 1987, where she continued advocating for sexual education. Her advocacy led to the Arkansas Legislature mandating a K-12 curriculum that included sex education and substance abuse prevention as well as programs to promote self-esteem. She also doubled childhood immunizations between 1987 and 1992, expanded Arkansas's prenatal care program, and increased home-care options for the chronically and terminally ill.

Elders's efforts led Clinton to appoint her as Surgeon General in 1993. Throughout her time as the head of the Arkansas State Department of Health, she had faced conservative backlash from her focus on sexual health. The backlash continued when she was nominated for Surgeon General. Thankfully, she was confirmed and was able to inspire more future doctors to achieve their dreams.

Elders's tenure as a public health director and as Surgeon General came in tandem with **Marilyn Gaston, MD**, who became the first Black woman director of a US Public Health Service bureau. In 1990, Gaston joined the Bureau of Primary Health Care in the US Health Resources and Services Administration. During her tenure, she focused on underserved families' health care. From 1990 to 2001, she and her staff presented new data from prophylactic penicillin programs carried out in Africa; this data highlighted the breadth Gaston's work in the area of penicillin. In fact, before becoming director, she was the author of a wide-ranging study in 1986 that showed how important long-term penicillin actually is in preventing septic infections in children with sickle cell disease. Gaston's study paved the way for Congress to pass legislation to fund nationwide SCD screening programs. That legislation had a spectacular effect within a year, since forty states had adopted screening programs.

There are so many people who could be added to this chapter. But there's one person whose name I want to shout out before we leave the scientific world of Black American history—**Chester Pierce, MD**, one of the pioneers who helped *Sesame Street* be what it is today.

Pierce, a psychiatrist, professor at Harvard Medical School, and founding president of the Black Psychiatrists of America, was brought onto the early developmental phase of *Sesame Street* in 1969. From his own work, he realized that the television had the power to shape children's perceptions of themselves. So, he advocated for the show to bring multiculturalism into homes across the country. Not only would this allow for children to become comfortable with a multicultural and multiracial America, it would provide children of color much-needed role models. Why was this necessary? Because, if we go back to the beauty chapter, where we learned about the doll tests carried out by psychologists **Kenneth and Mamie Clark**, the images and messages we receive can affect how we think about ourselves.

Sesame Street positively influenced the lives of children throughout the generations, including my own. I, like so many children, was able to see people who resembled me being treated with respect and kindness. As Pierce is quoted as saying in 1972, "Early childhood specialists have a staggering responsibility in producing planetary citizens whose geographic and intellectual provinces are as limitless as their all-embracing humanity."

Pierce didn't just bring a multicultural *Sesame Street* to children. In his collegiate years, he became the first

Black student to play in a major college football game at an all-White university below the Mason-Dixon line, when Harvard played against the University of Virginia. He also met with NASA, counseling them on how to bring American astronauts and Russian astronauts together within the Space Station. Once again, he was bringing the gap between cultures to provide understanding.

Black Scientific Excellence

There is a wealth of Black experiences within the US scientific industry. Many Black professionals in the sciences were treated to undignified racism, sexism, and prejudice of all sorts. And yet, they rose above and beyond to serve Americans of all stripes.

I am glad that the generations of Black STEM practitioners have made it possible for others to see themselves in this branch of study. For many Black burgeoning scientists and engineers, that means that they can imagine themselves as being the inventors of cures for diseases, technology that can help countries, and as the creators of expeditions to worlds unknown.

Chapter 8

Black Athleticism

America loves sports. We pay beaucoup money for NBA and NFL tickets, will fight our families over rival teams, and, in the case of my father, wear the shirts of teams who beat the University of Alabama football team just to mess with coworkers.

In today's society, America's sports culture is dominated by Black players. From baseball to basketball, from football to tennis and even golf, we have Black Americans who are excelling at the height of their game. We know all about stars like **Michael Jordan**, **LeBron James**, **Serena Williams**, **Venus Williams**, **Tiger Woods**, **Barry Bonds**, **Ken Griffey Jr.**, and many others. But what about some of the legends who paved the way for these stars? Let's go down memory lane to give the sports pioneers their due.

Barrier Breakers

In order for us to look up to athletes like LeBron James, the Williams sisters and others, there had to be people who broke the color barrier. They had the tough job of dealing with racism in order to showcase that Black people can and should be playing alongside their

White counterparts in a desegregated society.

Someone we know well is **Jackie Robinson.** You might recall that the Black Panther himself, Chadwick Boseman, had his breakout starring role as Robinson in the 2013 biopic 42. Incredibly, I was able to see parts of 42 get filmed since they did some of the principal

filming in downtown Birmingham. (I also tried to be an extra for that film, but that's a story for another day.) Through a series of ironic events, I was able to get a glimpse of the set—a glimpse of the world Robinson lived in. This world might have had cool cars and nostalgic ambiance, but his era was also segregated. Robinson's career, therefore, was a bridge between the old way and the new.

Robinson knew about the South's racism well. Born in Georgia to sharecroppers, Robinson, his mother, and his four siblings were the only Black family on their block. Robinson must have had to learn how to be tough against vitriol, which would serve him well in his future career as one of the most important baseball players in America.

Robinson was always gifted in sports; while attending UCLA, he became the first athlete to win varsity letters in four sports, including basketball, football, track, and, of course, baseball. He was also named to the All-American football team, but, unfortunately, Robinson had to leave college due to financial issues and enlisted in the army. Again, he showed excellence, advancing to second lieutenant. However, he was court-martialed for refusing to move to the back of an army bus. He was eventually acquitted, and, after some time as an army athletics coach, he received an honorable discharge.

Thankfully, a career in the army didn't work out, since we wouldn't have gotten Robinson's rise to sports prominence within the Negro Baseball League. He played with the league for two years, leading to Brooklyn Dodgers president Branch Rickey reaching out to Robinson about joining his team in 1947. The move was, as we know, historic; he was the first baseball player to break the color barrier within the sport and had to fight against racism from baseball fans nationwide.

Regardless of the pushback, he ended his rookie year with the title of National League Rookie of the Year, and, in 1949, he was named the league's Most Valuable Player of the Year. By 1962, he had become a new inductee to the Baseball Hall of Fame.

While we know tons about Robinson, there are plenty of pioneers we don't know a lot about, such as **Kenny Washington**, the first Black NFL player in the modern era. Washington was one of Robinson's teammates when they both played baseball at UCLA, so it's ironic that both of them would go on to create sports history. However, his claim to fame is football. While at UCLA, he played for the UCLA Bruins, winning the Douglas Fairbanks trophy as the best college football player in the country. In 1940, he was also named to an American college all-star team.

Even though Robinson was the first Black baseball player in the major leagues, the lack of Black players largely seemed like a societal, understood boundary that had yet to be crossed. On the flip side, the NFL had set an industry-wide ban against Black football players in 1933. So, instead of trying out for the NFL, Washington became a Los Angeles police officer. Going into policework was probably an easy sell for Washington, since his uncle was the highest-ranking Black officer in the department. But throughout his policing, he played football. During WWII, he played minor league football part-time, but this move resulted in Washington ruining the cartilage in his knees.

Thankfully, his knee injuries didn't hinder him from becoming an NFL pioneer. Once the NFL abolished their racist ban on Black players in 1945, the Cleveland Rams were relocated to Los Angeles and were required to sign Black players or risk losing their lease on the LA Memorial Coliseum. This led Washington to become their first signee, the first Black player to sign an NFL contract in the NFL's postwar era. **Woodrow Strode**, another of Robinson and Washington's teammates from UCLA, was also signed to the Rams two months later.

So, what about Washington's knees? Well, surgery helped Washington play for three seasons before he retired in 1948. But even though his career was short, Washington ushered in a new era in the NFL, one that is as remarkable as it is contentious, as we'll see later on in the chapter.

However, one of the athletes affected by Washington's historic career was **Ernie Davis**, a two-time All-

American from Syracuse University. Davis was the first Black recipient of the Heisman Trophy, the highest honor for a college football player. He was also awarded the Walter Camp Memorial Trophy, after which President John F. Kennedy, a fan, asked to meet him personally. He then went on to become the number one pick in the 1961 NFL Draft. Sadly, Davis died at only twenty-three years old from leukemia in 1963, but in his short life, he made a big impact.

Davis's career was also swayed by **Jim Brown**, who initially convinced Davis to attend Brown's alma mater, Syracuse, since he felt it would be more welcoming to a young Black athlete like Davis. In Syracuse, he earned the nickname "The Elmira Express" because of his childhood town of Elmira, New York, and because he would body people on the field. During his sophomoric career with Syracuse, Davis made ten touchdowns and rushed 686 yards.

When Davis was drafted into the NFL, he was originally signed to Washington but was quickly traded to the Cleveland Browns, the same team Brown himself played for between 1957 to 1965. Davis was given the largest contract to a rookie at that time in history—a three-year, sixty-five thousand dollar contract.

It might be unthinkable to some, especially younger people, that the NBA could have ever had a racial barrier against Black players. But it did, and that barrier was broken by the league's first Black players **Earl Lloyd**, **Nat "Sweetwater" Clifton**, and **Chuck Cooper** in 1950.

Lloyd was the first Black American to play in an NBA game as a member of the Washington Capitols. Cooper, on the other hand, was the first Black American to be drafted to the NBA. Clifton became the first Black American player to sign an NBA contract.

Perhaps it's evident that the NBA had an easier time accepting their Black players than other sports leagues, seeing how the debuts of Cooper, Clifton, and Lloyd weren't met with the same vitriol as Robinson's was when he went to the major leagues. First of all, the NBA invited these three men within the same year, allowing them to share the burden of "basketball pioneer" instead of putting the stress all on one person. In fact, when the NBA interviewed Lloyd about his time in the NBA before his death in 2015, he said his time in the league wasn't comparable to Robinson's within baseball, saying that because college basketball was already integrated, there was "a different mentality" regarding the sport.

However, he did say that he experienced racism in certain places where his team traveled to. In some cities, he couldn't eat or sleep with his teammates. But he said something that all of us should be mindful of when facing discrimination: "If you let yourself become bitter, it will eat away at you inside. If adversity doesn't kill you, it makes you a better person."

It's thanks to these pioneers that we began to see more Black legendary players rise in the ranks. For instance, current basketball stars are trying to live up to the legacies of **Wilt Chamberlain** and **Bill Russell**, considered two of the league's best-ever players who revolutionized the sport in the 1960s and 1970s. For instance, in Chamberlain's career, the NBA had to change rules regarding lane widening, inbounding the ball, free throw shooting, and creating offensive goaltending. And in the 1965–66 season, Russell became player-coach for his team, the Boston Celtics, becoming the first African American NBA coach.

If we take a detour back to Robinson's career in baseball, one such person he paved the way for is **Willie Mays**, who has a Birmingham connection as well. He started out his baseball career with the Birmingham Black Barons, one of the best teams in the Negro Baseball League, and I'm not just saying that because I'm a Birminghamian. The Black Barons had some of the best players, including Mobile, Alabama, native **Leroy "Satchel" Paige**. Paige was one of the stars of the Negro Leagues, playing with multiple teams (for the best pay), but particularly for the Kansas City Monarchs. Again, there's a Robinson connection, since Robinson also played for the Monarchs when he was a part of the Negro Leagues. Paige went onto play for the major leagues with the Cleveland Indians in 1948 at the age of forty-two, an age at which most athletes would be considering retirement.

While Paige entered the major leagues as an elder statesman of baseball, Mays started in the Negro Leagues at age sixteen, allowing him to start his career with the New York Giants in 1950 at the still-young age of nineteen. Just like Robinson, Mays was named the NL Rookie of the Year and helped his team tie with the Dodgers at the end of a 1951 season, erasing the Giants' thirteen-game deficit.

After that, Mays spent two years in the army, but he came back to the Giants in 1954, taking his team to glory once again. Mays ended his time with the Giants as a two-time NL MVP and a twenty-time all-star after twenty-one seasons; he played a final season of baseball between 1972 and 1973 with the New York Mets. He also had the second most home runs ever at the time of his retirement, leading in home runs four separate times.

Hank Aaron, another Mobile native, was given this stellar accolade from legendary boxer and activist Muhammad Ali—"The only man I idolize more than myself." High praise, indeed.

Aaron also played with the Negro Leagues, but his time in the Negro and minor leagues were short lived. His career really began when he signed with the Milwaukee Braves. He became one of the league's stars, earning three Gold Glove Awards and twenty-five all-star appearances. In 1957, thought to be his best season of baseball, he hit forty-four home runs and earned the National League MVP Award. His efforts led the Braves to their first World Series Championship since 1914. In 1974, he beat Babe Ruth's 714 home runs, earning 755 home runs. He kept the record until 2007.

We've talked a lot about Robinson's impact in the world of sports, but the concept of a Black sports superstar wouldn't even be in existence if it wasn't for **Marshall "Major" Taylor**. This little-known athlete has slowly gotten the recognition he deserves decades after his death. Not only did he break the color barrier in the sport, he also became the first Black American world champion ever.

Taylor was born in Indiana in 1878 and assisted his father, who worked in the coach house of a rich family. Taylor and the family's son became friends, and he was weirdly hired as the boy's official companion. At least they were actually friends in real life. Also, it's not as if Taylor didn't receive something for his trouble as a hired companion; he was given private tutoring, clothing, and, most importantly for our story, his very first bicycle.

When the rich family moved to Chicago, Taylor's mother wanted him to remain with her. The family was initially reluctant to do that, but they complied with the wish of Taylor's mother. However, it seems like Taylor himself wasn't particularly happy with the decision, since he wrote that he was taken from "the happy life of a millionaire kid to that of a common errand boy." To earn money for his family, he worked at a bicycle shop and attracted customers by doing stunts in an army uniform. This earned him the nickname, "Major."

Major's first race, at thirteen years old, was one he didn't even apply for. His employer entered him without Taylor's knowledge, and it was only done as a publicity stunt. But he won the race, beginning his career as an athlete. He held seven world records by 1898, and, by 1900, he was named the National Cycling Champion. He was sponsored by Iver Johnson Arms and Cycle Works throughout his 1900 season and his overseas touring. This is just one of the perks

Taylor received as one of the highest-paid athletes. He earned the second nickname "The Black Cyclone" because of his prowess, but also because of his race. In fact, racial mockery and discrimination was a huge part of what Taylor had to endure, including being banned from a track in his hometown of Indianapolis because he beat the other White cyclists and broke two world records.

Sadly, after Taylor retired in 1910, he fell out of common knowledge and died lonely and penniless in a Chicago hospital in 1932. Even his self-published autobiography, *The Fastest Bicycle Ride in the World*, fell into obscurity because, by that point, America was over the novelty of bicycles. His grave was even unmarked, unfit for a sports legend. Thankfully, in 1940, former bicycle professionals used money donated by Frank Schwinn to relocate Taylor's remains to a burial site more befitting a sports revolutionary in Illinois. In the 1980s, Taylor was finally inducted into the Bicycling Hall of Fame.

Similarly, like Robinson, we are knowledgeable of **Jesse Owens**, the track and field star who challenged Adolf Hitler's idea of the perfect "Aryan" race by defeating German athletes at the 1936 Berlin Olympics. Owens became the biggest Olympic star of his day, earning four gold medals and the admiration of the nation. But before Owens's historic performance, there was another Black Olympian who paved the way for Black Olympians after him, **John Taylor**.

Taylor was born in 1882 as a well-off child; his father was a successful businessman in Washington DC. He continued living the high life after his family moved to Pennsylvania and he attended Philadelphia's elite Central High School.

It was at Central High that Taylor became invested in track and field and was chosen as the track team captain. He excelled in the field, becoming the interscholastic quarter-mile champ for two years straight. He also graduated in 1902 with the title of best quarter-mile runner in Philadelphia. He continued his prestigious resume in both track and academics by attending Brown Prep, where he was named the best prep quarter-miler in the country. When he went to the University of Pennsylvania in 1903, he won the Intercollegiate Association of Amateur Athletes of America championship, setting a new meet record for the quarter mile.

By 1904, Taylor was traveling across the globe to Europe, competing (and winning) most of his matches in England and France. When 1905 rolled around, he actually took a break from running to focus on what he wanted to do in his academic life. He reentered the University of Pennsylvania after withdrawing from Wharton and majored in veterinary medicine. However, by 1906, he was back to running, and Penn's new coach, Mike Murphy, put Taylor on the path toward the 1908 Olympics. His spot on the Olympic team made him the first African American to represent the country in an international competition. He came away from the meet as the first Black American to win a gold medal.

Sadly, his trip to England, where the Olympics were being held, led to Taylor's demise. He was having trouble competing in his races because of England's damp conditions. When he came back home, he developed typhoid pneumonia and died at just twenty-six years old, four months after winning his historic gold medal.

However, his success provided a path for Jesse Owens as well as **Alice Coachman**, who became the first Black American woman to win an Olympic gold medal in 1948.

The track and field star earned her historic gold in London in the high jump finals when she set a world record of jumping a height of five feet, six and an eighth inches. This feat probably wasn't imaginable for many who lived around her in Albany, Georgia, where she was born and raised as one of ten children. She grew up being denied opportunities to train and compete. So she trained by running on dirt roads and fields and used old equipment to help her with her track and field techniques.

In 1939, at just sixteen years old, she earned a scholarship to Tuskegee Institute, now called Tuskegee University, in Tuskegee, Alabama. Clearly, Tuskegee knew talent when they saw it, since before leaving high school, she broke the high school and college high jump records in the Amateur Athlete Union National Championship. And she did it barefoot.

When she attended Albany State College in 1946, she became the national champion in the 50- and 100-meter races as well as the 400-meter relay and the high jump. When she arrived as an Olympic delegate in London in 1948, she wasn't at her finest form—she had a back injury. Yet, she set her world record anyway. Incredibly, she is quoted as saying she didn't even know she had won the gold until she was on her way to accept her award and saw her name on the board.

After making history, she went back to Albany State to complete her degree and officially retire from sports. Despite that, she was the first Black American to earn an endorsement deal once Coca-Cola asked her to become their spokesperson.

Coachman didn't just utilize her stardom for money-making ventures, though; she used it to pay it forward. Years later, she established the Alice Coachman Track and Field Foundation to help retired Olympians as well as provide support to younger athletes as they work to achieve Olympic dreams.

Naturally, she has been inducted into several Halls of Fame, including the National Track & Field Hall of Fame and the US Olympic Hall of Fame. She also became the first woman to receive the Silver Anniversary Award from the National Collegiate Athletic Association.

She's also named as one of the 100 greatest Olympians in history. And to think it all started on dirt roads and fields in Georgia.

Debi Thomas brought Black Excellence to the ice rink when she became the first Black American athlete to earn at medal at the Winter Olympics. Incredibly, this acknowledgement happened in 1988. For reference, the Winter Olympics were established in 1924. So, clearly, a medal was long overdue.

Thomas has several championships under her belt, finishing second and winning the senior title at the US Nationals in 1985, winning the 1986 world championship and bronze at the 1988 World Championships. She has also been inducted into the US Figure Skating Hall of Fame and, after graduating Northwestern Medical School, became an orthopedic surgeon. But despite all of these accomplishments, she eventually became broke and lived in a trailer. Also, as much as I love Iyanla Vanzant, perhaps the last place you want to be on is *Iyanla: Fix My Life*. And yet, that's where Thomas wound up, trying to pick up the pieces, which include her struggles with bipolar disorder.

You might be wondering what's become of Thomas since her downward turn. According to the *New York Post*, she doesn't have any regrets about her path. "It may look [to] people on the outside like it's insane, but I don't care," she said. "I don't care about living in a trailer. People are so obsessed with material things, but I only care about knowledge."

That might be true, but as someone who herself has a history with mental illness, my biggest hope is that Thomas finds a way to get proper help.

On a lighter note, **Althea Gibson** transformed the tennis world by becoming the first African American superstar in women's tennis. A Harlem native, she came from meager beginnings and rose to the top of the tennis profession via the Black tennis circuit, the American Tennis Association. After winning several competitions, including ten championships back to back between 1947 and 1956, she was finally able to turn pro in 1959 after receiving tons of pushback in previous years from the segregated tennis circuit. Her moment to enter came in 1950, when former number one tennis player Alice Mable wrote a scathing letter in *American Lawn Tennis* magazine about her profession's prejudice, particularly when it came to barring Gibson from the pro league. Fast forward to 1959, when she was finally able to live out her dreams of playing professionally.

In between the time of Mable's letter and Gibson turning pro, Gibson continued to show why she should be seen as a professional player. She became the first African American ever to play at Wimbledon in 1951. Within a year, she became a Top Ten player in the country. In 1953, she went up to number seven and by 1955, she was traveling around the world to compete thanks to a sponsorship by the United States Lawn Tennis Association. By 1956, she won the French Open and, the following two years, she won at Wimbledon and the US Open. In total, Gibson had won fifty-six singles and doubles championships before actually turning pro. She already had a resume that only Serena and Venus Williams have been able to rival today.

Something we don't hear too much about, though, is Gibson's professional golfing career. Again, she made history in the 1960s as the first African American golfer in the women's pro golf tour. But her tennis career is what has earned her the most recognition, and she was finally inducted into the International Tennis

Hall of Fame in 1971. Four years later, she took on a new career as the Commissioner of Athletics for New Jersey, a position she held for ten years. She also held a position on the governor's council on physical fitness.

Even though she was a pioneer in her sport, Gibson didn't consider herself a leader. In fact, she wrote in her 1958 autobiography, "I have never regarded myself as a crusader. I don't consciously beat the drums for any cause, not even the negro in the United States."

While she might not have considered herself in a revolutionary light, she is, in fact, someone who has made it possible for the Williams sisters, Sloane Stephens, Coco Gauff, and others to dominate the sport and inspire others to pick up a racket and play. These players not only excelled in sports, they spoke out as activists, reveling in their ability to make change with their notoriety.

Leading Athlete-Activists

While it is true that America is a sports-loving country, we are also a nation that, to this day, wrestles with the blurred lines between sports and civil rights advocacy. We've seen it recently with how former NFL star Colin Kaepernick was blackballed by the NFL for taking a knee on the field. His hope was to raise awareness about police brutality against vulnerable Black Americans.

But should Black sports players "stick to sports," as many critics have charged, when their people are being gunned down? Personally, I don't think so. Thankfully, there are plenty of activists, including athlete-activists, who also disagree.

Who are some of the activists you need to know? There are plenty to choose from nowadays, such as **LeBron James**, who constantly speaks out against injustice and uses his clout and money to give back to his hometown of Akron, Ohio, including building an elementary school called the I Promise School.

There is **Serena Williams**, who has preached the values of feminism and equality through her stellar tennis career and in her work off the court. And there's one athlete who paved the way for them and others when it comes to activism: **Arthur Ashe**.

Ashe broke through the racial barriers in the tennis world by becoming the first Black American chosen to play in the Davis Cup in the United States. He was also the first Black American male to win the US Open in 1968, the Australian Open in 1970, and Wimbledon in 1975. Within ten years of representing the US in the Davis Cup, he helped America win five championships between 1963 and 1978.

Ashe combined his sports prowess with his activism, speaking out against civil rights violations, particularly after the assassinations of Martin Luther King Jr. and President John F. Kennedy. Part of his outspoken persona came from a sense of shame for not speaking up in the years prior. He also began speaking out against Apartheid in South Africa, working with Harry Belafonte to create Artists and Athletes Against Apartheid. He was once arrested for protesting outside of the South African Embassy in Washington DC.

Ashe's activism grew to include gender equity, proper treatment for Haitian refugees, and eventually the AIDS epidemic after he contracted the disease due to a blood transfusion. He spent his last ten months speaking out for AIDS awareness, including addressing the World Health Organization on World AIDS Day in 1992. Ashe died in 1993 but left a legacy of activism behind him.

The 1968 Olympics might have been a normal Olympics meet if it wasn't for the assassinations of King and Kennedy. Plus, protests against the Vietnam War were beginning to become more mainstream. These events rocked the country and propelled many people to take up activism, such as in the case of Ashe. **Tommie Smith** and **John Carlos**, two track and field stars for the US, also used the limelight to highlight the turbulence that was happening in their home country.

The two stars were able to utilize the Olympics to their advantage because of their athletic talent; Smith won the gold for the 200 meter run, and Carlos won bronze. Since they realized they'd have the world looking at them, they agreed to use the moment to highlight the

Black Power movement, which had arisen because of many Black Americans' frustrations with the civil rights movement's penchant for accepting incremental movements of the needle.

The Black Power movement, on the other hand, was about actively fighting racism and pushed for more impactful changes rather than changes that would be deemed acceptable by the mainstream. It also advocated for Black nationalism and racial pride. While pride in one's race is one thing, there's a lot that could be said about Black nationalism, and this topic is way too heady to get into in this book. But on the whole, the Black Power movement can be summed up in the classic phrase, "I'm Black and proud."

At the 1968 Olympics, the two athletes took to the podium during their medal ceremony and raised their fists in the air as the National Anthem played. The fists encapsulated all of the societal and political animus the two players were feeling, and the White Australian silver medalist who was on the podium next to them, Peter Norman, stood with them in solidarity. Unfortunately, this show of political activism took a toll on all three of the runners' careers. At least Carlos and Smith were eventually able to return to their running careers several years after the 1968 Olympics. But Norman, who stood in solidarity in part because of Australia's own racist policies, was never welcomed back into the fold. He died in 2006 without ever getting a formal apology or acknowledgement of his contributions to the sport. The Australian government's apology came six years later, in 2012, but frankly, that's six years too late. However, Smith and Carlos seemed to remain his friends; they were pallbearers at his funeral.

Also, while at the 1968 Olympics, Carlos and Smith helped create the Olympic Project for Human Rights, an organization that wanted to use the Olympics as an opportunity to demand better treatment for Black athletes and the Black diaspora as a whole. Some of the group's demands included hiring more Black coaches and compelling the Olympics to rescind their invitations to Apartheid-ridden South Africa and Rhodesia.

Meanwhile, in boxing, **Muhammad Ali** kept making history as "The Greatest" heavyweight champion—and he would tell you, too, since he was all about positive self-promotion. But his political life was just as infamous as his boxing career. Born Cassius Clay, he converted to the Nation of Islam in 1964. Many Black Americans were converted to Islam at that time, specifically the Nation of Islam's brand of Islamic teaching. However, due to its political nature, this was rather controversial. How controversial? *Extremely.* Again, a book could be made about the Nation all on its own. But Ali seemingly

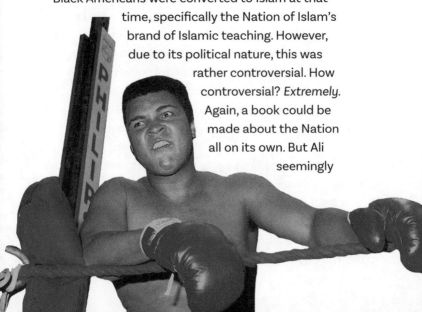

converted because of his political views. As a result, he also cited his religious beliefs as his reason for refusing to serve the US Army during the Vietnam War.

While Ali made a lot of social and political stands against racism and injustice, this is probably one of the moments that got him in the most trouble with the government. In fact, he was arrested for not serving in the war, and the New York State Athletic Commission revoked his heavyweight belt and had his boxing license suspended. He was convicted of draft evasion and was given the maximum sentence of five years in prison and a ten thousand dollar fine.

Throughout the time he appealed the conviction, he was free, but he wasn't idle during his three-year boxing ban. He spent the time campaigning against the war and speaking at college campuses. And, as it would seem, he was one of the few in the country who saw the writing on the wall when it came to the Vietnam War. Eventually, public sentiment toward the war turned cold, and the unpopular status he engendered by avoiding the war faded away. More and more people began supporting Ali again, and in 1970, the New York Supreme Court ordered for Ali's boxing license to get reinstated. In 1971, the US Supreme Court overturned his draft dodging conviction with a unanimous vote.

Later on, his daughter **Laila Ali** also broke her own barriers as a female boxer, retiring with an incredible 24-0 record. But while she made her own way in sports, she also continued her father's legacy of activism by writing her memoir *Reach!: Finding Strength, Spirit and Personal Power* as a motivator for her fans. She was also the president—and is the current trustee—of the Women's Sports Foundation, a nonprofit founded by tennis legend Billie Jean King to empower girls and women through the character-building avenue of sports.

What would some of these activists say about Kaepernick? Well, Carlos and Smith, who continue to be friends today, are behind him, offering their own solidarity to him and other athletes who are activists for the human condition. "What I did was right forty-eight years ago, and forty-eight years later it has proven to be right," said Carlos to *The Telegraph* in 2016. "In 1968, we were on a program for humanity—we are still on the same program today."

I'm sure if Ali were alive—he died from Parkinson's disease in 2016—he would agree, since he continued to devote his life to activism. Incredibly, he met with then-Iraqi leader Saddam Hussein in 1990 to negotiate the release of American hostages. In 2002, he was a United Nations Messenger of Peace, traveling to Afghanistan to spread the message of a united world. In 2005, after earning the Presidential Medal of Freedom, he opened the Muhammad Ali Center. The cultural center and nonprofit prides itself on social responsibility and peace.

And, as we can tell from how much Ashe regretted not speaking out against injustices earlier, I feel he would consider Kaepernick extremely brave for standing his ground. It takes a special person to put their career on the line. Thankfully that person will also realize that there are bigger, greater things at stake than money and fame.

Athletic Dreams, Societal Progress

Hopefully, what we've learned is how much sports do matter in the realm of American history and culture. The same political and societal junk that was affecting Black Americans in other realms of life were affecting these athletes too. Thankfully, they were able to rise above the junk and achieve greatness—the kind that might have seemed unachievable. Not only that, but they showed future athletes of color that they, too, could achieve their wildest dreams. All they had to do was have the heart to see things through.

THE BOOK OF

Awesome

BLACK
AMERICANS

Epilogue

You've made it to the end of our journey together through Black American history. Hopefully, you've come away from it even more enlightened and inspired by the movers and shakers who made America what it is today.

However, this is certainly not the end of the complete journey. Take your knowledge and expand on it. I was only able to cover a small portion of each individual's life; it's up to you to start your own journey and learn more about the people in this book who inspire you the most.

Aside from continuing your own research party, find ways to educate others about what you've learned. You don't have to do things overtly, but just a simple conversation starter can introduce someone else to how much Black American history interacts with us on a daily basis. Like, if you're at a red light with your mom or dad, you could simply say, "Hey, did you know a Black inventor named Garrett Morgan invented the stop light?" Or, if you're learning about Rosa Parks in class, you could raise your hand and say, "May we also learn about Claudette Colvin?" Who knows? Just by raising your voice, you could inspire someone to learn more about a subject they didn't know a lot about.

Apart from passing it forward, make sure to apply any of the lessons you've learned from this book in your own life. You might want to start speaking up for causes or individuals you hold dear like Arthur Ashe, or perhaps you simply want to create your own garden like Ron Finley. Maybe you want to start attending protests like Marsha P. Johnson and Miss Major. Or maybe you want to look up at the stars and start your own astronomy projects like Benjamin Banneker, Mae Jemison, and others.

What's great about Black American history is that it's still being written. There are new civil rights leaders within the ranks of Dream Defenders and Black Lives Matter. There are new sports activists such as LeBron James and the Williams sisters. There are new LGBTQ activists like actress Laverne Cox and singer Janelle Monáe. Regardless of the industry or field, there is someone new who is pushing society forward.

That also includes you.

You are part of Black history as well, so I need you to do one simple thing: Go out and accomplish your gift to the world. Go out and be proud, Black, and talented. Make your mark in history, because someone, like me, will be around to record it.

Bibliography

"1898 Alfred Teen Blackburn-Slave, Civil War, Document."
WorthPoint. [Online] Available https://www.worthpoint.com/
worthopedia/1898-alfred-teen-blackburn-slave-129044928.

"1969: Fannie Lou Hamer Founds Freedom Farm Cooperative."
The SNCC Legacy Project and Duke University Libraries [Online]
https://snccdigital.org/events/fannie-lou-hamer-founds-
freedom-farm-cooperative/.

Abigail Higgins. "40 Years a Slave: The Extraordinary Tale of an African
Prince Stolen from his Kingdom." History [Online] Available https://
www.history.com/news/african-prince-slavery-abdulrahman-
ibrahim-ibn-sori, February 8, 2019.

"About Benjamin Banneker." Benjamin Banneker, Inc. [Online]
Available http://banneker1753.com/benjamin-banneker/.

"About EJI." The Legacy Museum and The National Memorial for
Peace and Justice [Online] Available https://museumandmemorial.
eji.org/about.

"About Iman." Iman Cosmetics [Online] Available https://
imancosmetics.com/pages/about-iman.

"About Medgar and Myrlie." Medgar & Myrlie Evers Institute [Online]
Available http://www.eversinstitute.org/about-medgar-myrlie/.

"About New Voices." New Voices Fund. Sundial Group [Online]
Available https://newvoicesfund.com/about/.

"About the Project: Introduction-The Need to Document Unsung
Foot Soldiers." The Foot Soldier Project for Civil Rights Studies at
the University of Georgia [Online] Available http://www.footsoldier.
uga.edu/about/intro.html, 2006.

"About The Reverend Absalom Jones..." The African Episcopal Church
of St. Thomas. [Online] Available *http://www.aecst.org/ajones.htm.*

"About Us." Carol's Daughter [Online] Available https://www.
carolsdaughter.com/about-us.html.

"About Us." Fashion Fair [Online] Available http://www.fashionfair.
com/aboutus.php.

"About Us." National Medical Association [Online] Available https://www.nmanet.org/page/About_Us.

"About USGBC." U.S. Green Building Council [Online] Available https://new.usgbc.org/about.

African American Registry. "Inventor Marie Van Brittan Brown born." African American Registry. [Online] Available https://aaregistry.org/story/inventor-marie-van-brittan-brown-born/.

African American Registry. "Tuskegee founder Lewis Adams born." [Online] Available https://aaregistry.org/story/tuskegee-founder-lewis-adams-born/.

Alan Hughes. "Meet the CEO Who Helped Reshape Atlanta's Skyline: Herman J. Russell." Black Enterprise [Online] Available https://www.blackenterprise.com/herman-j-russell-atlanta-developer-skyline/ July 25, 2014.

Alexander Klein. "Beverly Johnson (1952–)." BlackPast [Online] Available https://www.blackpast.org/african-american-history/johnson-beverly-1952/, December 17, 2010.

"Alice Coachman—Athletics." The International Olympic Committee [Online] Available https://www.olympic.org/news/alice-coachman-athletics.

Alice Kurima Newberry. "8 Black Environmentalists You Need To Know." Greenpeace [Online] Available https://www.greenpeace.org/usa/8-black-environmentalists-need-know/, February 6, 2018.

Amy Feldman. "How A Single Mom Battling Breast Cancer Built Beauty Bakerie To A $5M Brand, Got Unilever To Invest." Forbes [Online] Available https://www.forbes.com/sites/amyfeldman/2017/12/03/how-a-single-mom-battling-breast-cancer-built-beauty-bakerie-to-a-5m-brand-got-unilever-to-invest/#79c078d143f8, December 3, 2017.

Ann Rayson. "Wright, Richard." American National Biography. Oxford University Press [Online] Available https://www.anb.org/view/10.1093/anb/9780198606697.001.0001/anb-9780198606697-e-1601806;jsessionid=C38B362249629DB3D71A21E85AF0133A.

Anne Harrington. "The Forgotten Tale of How Black Psychiatrists

Helped Make 'Sesame Street.' " Undark Magazine. Daily Beast [Online] Available https://www.thedailybeast.com/chester-pierce-the-forgotten-tale-of-how-a-black-psychiatrist-helped-make-sesame-street?source=articles&via=rss, May 19, 2019.

Ansley Wegner. "Cooper, Anna Julia."NCPedia [Online] Available https://ncpedia.org/biography/cooper-anna-julia-haywood, 2010.

Anuja Vaidya. "Dr. Patrice Harris becomes first black female president of American Medical Association." Becker's Hospital Review [Online] Available https://www.beckershospitalreview.com/hospital-executive-moves/dr-patrice-harris-becomes-first-black-president-of-american-medical-association.html, June 11, 2019.

Arlisha Norwood. "Dorothy Height." National Women's History Museum [Online] Available https://www.womenshistory.org/education-resources/biographies/dorothy-height, 2017.

Arlisha R. Norwood. "Ida B. Wells." National Women's History Museum [Online] Available https://www.womenshistory.org/education-resources/biographies/ida-b-wells-barnett, 2017.

Arlisha R. Norwood. "Maggie L. Walker." National Women's History Museum [Online] Available https://www.womenshistory.org/education-resources/biographies/maggie-l-walker, 2017.

Arlisha R. Norwood. "Wilma Rudolph." National Women's History Museum [Online] Available https://www.womenshistory.org/education-resources/biographies/wilma-rudolph, 2017.

"Arthur Ashe." International Tennis Hall of Fame [Online] Available https://www.tennisfame.com/hall-of-famers/inductees/arthur-ashe.

"Artist Biography." The Gordon Parks Foundation [Online] Available http://www.gordonparksfoundation.org/artist/biography.

"Astronaut Mae Jemison." NASA [Online] Available https://www.nasa.gov/audience/forstudents/k-4/home/F_Astronaut_Mae_Jemison.html, April 1, 2004.

"Attorneys & Staff." Land Loss Prevention Project [Online] Available https://www.landloss.org/staff.html.

Associated Press. "Edith Jones, who integrated southern medical schools, dies." NBC News [Online] Available https://www.nbcnews. com/news/nbcblk/edith-jones-who-integrated-southern-medical-schools-dies-n1031811?cid=sm_npd_nn_tw_ma, July 19, 2019.

Ayman Tarek Elkholy. "Ayuba Suleiman Diallo (1701-1773). BlackPast. [Online] Available https://www.blackpast.org/global-african-history/diallo-ayuba-suleiman-1701-1773/, April 26, 2019

Barbara Reynolds. "Betty and Coretta: Debunking the drama in Lifetime's TV movie about the two widowed legends." *The Washington Post* [Online] Available https://www.washingtonpost. com/blogs/therootdc/post/betty-and-coretta-debunking-the-drama-in-lifetimes-tv-movie-about-the-two-widowed-legends/2013/02/01/1b7344f0-6c78-11e2-8740-9b58f43c191a_blog.html?noredirect=on&utm_term=.49f8b73b5e87, February 1, 2013.

"Bayard Rustin." Quakers in the World [Online] Available http://www. quakersintheworld.org/quakers-in-action/160/Bayard-Rustin.

"Benjamin Banneker (1731-1806). Brookhaven National Laboratory. [Online] Available https://www.bnl.gov/bera/activities/globe/banneker.htm.

"Bessie Smith." Rock & Roll Hall of Fame [Online] Available https:// www.rockhall.com/inductees/bessie-smith.

"Bessie Smith." University of Illinois Springfield [Online] Available https://www.uis.edu/gendersexualitystudentservices/bessiesmith/.

"Beverly Wright, Ph.D., Executive DIrector." Deep South Center For Environmental Justice [Online] Available http://www.dscej.org/our-story/our-team/beverly-l-wright-phd.

"Biography of Archer Alexander." Black History Now [Online] Available http://blackhistorynow.com/archer-alexander/, April 27, 2013.

"Biography." Dr. Robert Bullard: Father of Environmental Justice [Online] Available https://drrobertbullard.com/biography/.

"Biography." JackieRobinson.com [Online] Available https://www. jackierobinson.com/biography/.

Biography.com Editors. "Alice Coachman Biography." Biography. [Online] Available https://www.biography.com/athlete/alice-coachman, July 29, 2014.

Biography.com Editors. "Alvin Ailey Biography." Biography [Online] Available https://www.biography.com/performer/alvin-ailey, April 27, 2017.

Biography.com Editors. "Bayard Rustin Biography." Biography [Online] Available https://www.biography.com/activist/bayard-rustin, April 2, 2014.

Biography.com Editors. "Claudette Colvin Biography." Biography [Online] Available https://www.biography.com/activist/claudette-colvin, January 19, 2018.

Biography.com Editors. "Diane Nash Biography." Biography [Online] Available https://www.biography.com/activist/diane-nash, January 25, 2018.

Biography.com Editors. "Fred Shuttlesworth Biography." Biography [Online] Available https://www.biography.com/activist/fred-shuttlesworth, January 19, 2015.

Biography.com Editors. "Jack Johnson Biography." Biography [Online] Available https://www.biography.com/athlete/jack-johnson, April 2, 2014.

Biography.com Editors. "James West Biography." Biography [Online] Available https://www.biography.com/inventor/james-west, January 19, 2018.

Biography.com Editors. "Laila Ali Biography." [Online] Available https://www.biography.com/athlete/laila-ali, April 2, 2014.

Biography.com Editors. "Ma Rainey." Biography [Online] Available https://www.biography.com/musician/ma-rainey, April 27, 2017.

Biography.com Editors. "Madam C.J. Walker Biography." Biography [Online] Available https://www.biography.com/inventor/madam-cj-walker, February 28, 2018.

Biography.com Editors. "Misty Copeland Biography." Biography [Online] Available https://www.biography.com/athlete/misty-copeland, January 19, 2018.

Biography.com Editors. "Otis Boykin Biography." Biography [Online] Available https://www.biography.com/inventor/otis-boykin, April 2, 2014.

Biography.com Editors. "Patricia Bath Biography." Biography. [Online] Available https://www.biography.com/scientist/patricia-bath, April 2, 2014.

Biography.com Editors. "Ralph D. Abernathy Biography." Biography [Online] Available https://www.biography.com/activist/ralph-d-abernathy, June 29, 2014.

Biography.com Editors. "Rosa Parks Biography." Biography [Online] Available https://www.biography.com/activist/rosa-parks, February 27, 2018.

Biography.com Editors. "Ruby Bridges Biography." Biography [Online] Available https://www.biography.com/activist/ruby-bridges, April 27, 2017.

Biography.com. Editors. "Solomon Northup Biography." Biography [Online] Available https://www.biography.com/writer/solomon-northup, January 7, 2015.

"Biography: Dr. Lonnie Johnson." Lonniejohnson.com [Online] Available https://www.lonniejohnson.com/biography/.

Birmingham Civil Rights Institute. "Birmingham Civil Rights Institute opens 'Foot Soldiers' exhibit." Alabama Newscenter [Online] Available https://alabamanewscenter.com/2018/04/18/birmingham-civil-rights-institute-opens-foot-soldiers-exhibit/, April 18, 2018.

"Blacks, Picnics and Lynchings—January 2004." Ferris State University [Online] https://www.ferris.edu/HTMLS/news/jimcrow/question/2004/january.htm, 2004.

"Board of Trustees." Women's Sports Foundation [Online] Available https://www.womenssportsfoundation.org/about-us/people/board-of-trustees/, Feb. 12, 2016.

"Board." Dreaming Out Loud Inc. [Online] Available http://dreamingoutloud.org/about/#board.

"Brands." Combs Enterprises. [Online] Available https://www.

combsenterprises.com/company-portfolio/.

"Bristow, Lonnie 1930—". *Contemporary Black Biography.*
Encyclopedia.com [Online] Available https://www.encyclopedia.
com/education/news-wires-white-papers-and-books/bristow-
lonnie-1930, 2005.

Cara Anthony. "A legacy reborn, Madam C.J. Walker hair products are
back." Indianapolis Star [Online] Available https://www.indystar.
com/story/life/2016/09/30/100-years-later-madam-c-j-walker-
hair-products-back/90316380/, September 30, 2016.

Carlynn Trout. "Dred Scott (1800?-1858)." The State Historical Society
of Missouri [Online] Available https://historicmissourians.shsmo.
org/historicmissourians/name/s/scottd/.

Carmen Rios. "Rebel Girls: Bessie Smith Was a Queer Pioneer, and
We're Finally Gonna Get to Talk About It." Autostraddle [Online]
Available https://www.autostraddle.com/rebel-girls-bessie-smith-
was-a-queer-pioneer-and-were-finally-gonna-get-to-talk-about-
it-283712/, April 1, 2015.

"Carrie Mae Weems Biography." Carrie Mae Weems [Online] Available
http://carriemaeweems.net/bio.html.

"Carrie Mae Weems." MacArthur Foundation [Online] Available
https://www.macfound.org/fellows/905/.

Cashmere Nicole. "Discover The Story Behind One Of The Worlds'
Favorite Black-Owned Beauty Brands." Beauty Bakerie [Online]
Available https://www.beautybakerie.com/blogs/ice-cream-
social/favorite-black-owned-beauty-brands, March 1, 2017.

Cashmere Nicole. "Sugar Homes." Beauty Bakerie [Online] Available
https://www.beautybakerie.com/pages/sugar-homes.

Chris Ott. "Archibald Grimke (1849-1930). BlackPast. [Online]
Available https://www.blackpast.org/african-american-history/
grimke-archibald-1849-1930/, March 12, 2007.

"Christensen, Donna Marie." Office of History, Art & Archives. U.S.
House of Representatives [Online] Available https://history.house.
gov/People/Detail/10930.

Christine Blackerby. "Kidnapping of Free People of Color." National

Archives [Online] Available https://education.blogs.archives. gov/2013/11/12/kidnapping-of-free-people-of-color/, November 12, 2013.

"Christopher Bradshaw." Ashoka Changemakers [Online] Available https://www.changemakers.com/users/christopher-bradshaw.

Clare O'Connor. "Founders Of Mented Cosmetics Become 15th, 16th Black Women Ever To Raise $1M Capital." Forbes [Online] Available https://www.forbes.com/sites/clareoconnor/2017/10/16/ founders-of-mented-cosmetics-become-15th-16th-black- women-ever-to-raise-1m-capital/#7b91baac501d, October 16, 2017.

Clinton Cox, Otha Richard Sullivan, Eleanora Tate, Brenda Wilkinson and Jim Haskins, Ed. "Dr. Alexander T. Augusta." *Black Stars of Civil War Times: African Americans Who Lived Their Dreams.* Hoboken, NJ: John Wiley & Sons, Inc., 2003.

CNN Library. "1963 Birmingham Church Bombing Fast Facts." CNN [Online] Available https://www.cnn.com/2013/06/13/us/1963- birmingham-church-bombing-fast-facts/index.html, September 7, 2018.

Courtney Connley. "Sean 'Diddy' Combs credits his success to a business lesson he learned at age 12." CNBC. [Online] Available https://www.cnbc.com/2017/09/27/diddy-credits-his-success-to- a-business-lesson-he-learned-at-age-12.html, September 27, 2017.

Dan Jones. "Meet Kenny Washington, the First Black NFL Player of the Modern Era." History [Online] Available https://www.history.com/ news/first-black-nfl-player, February 2, 2018.

David A. Tomar. "Anna Julia Haywood Cooper: The Mother of Black Feminism." The Best Schools [Online] Available https:// thebestschools.org/magazine/anna-julia-haywood-cooper- mother-black-feminism/.

Debra Michals. "Madam C.J. Walker." National Women's Hisotry Museum [Online] Available https://www.womenshistory.org/ education-resources/biographies/madam-cj-walker, 2015.

Debra Michals. "Ruby Bridges." National Women's History Museum [Online] Available https://www.womenshistory.org/education-

resources/biographies/ruby-bridges?gclid=CjwKCAjwue3nBRACEi
wAkpZhmftu4mcXKnWM3RfhR9I3U20m-F2BAQ6d66ME1g48yMl
yjMmZS4LQyhoCtP4QAvD_BwE, 2015.

Debra Michals, Ed. "Mary McLeod Bethune." National Women's
History Museum [Online] Available https://www.womenshistory.
org/education-resources/biographies/mary-mcleod-bethune,
2015.

Deirdre Smith. "Black History Month: Chantel Johnson draws
inspiration from activist Fannie Lou Hamer." *Salisbury Post* [Online]
https://www.salisburypost.com/2019/02/06/black-history-
month-chantel-johnson-draws-inspiration-from-voting-and-
womens-rights-activist-fannie-lou-hamer/, February 6, 2019.

Denise Bergmeister, Rebecca Hund, Purvi Parikh. "Hannah Crafts."
Recovering 19th-Century American Women Writers. [Online]
Available https://blogs.stockton.edu/litrecovery/hannah-crafts/,
2015

"Denmark Vesey." PBS. [Online] https://www.pbs.org/thisfarbyfaith/
people/denmark_vesey.html, 2003.

"Destiny Watford: 2016 Goldman Prize Recipient North America."
The Goldman Environmental Prize [Online] Available https://www.
goldmanprize.org/recipient/destiny-watford/, 2016.

Devon Bailey: Co-Founder, Co-Executive Director, Director of Site &
Development [Online] Available http://www.phillyurbancreators.
org/devon-bailey.

"Diane Nash." The SNCC Legacy Project and Duke University Libraries
[Online] Available https://snccdigital.org/people/diane-nash-
bevel/.

Dominique Norman. "Black Excellence: Donyale Norman." V
Magazine [Online] Available https://vmagazine.com/article/black-
excellence-donyale-luna/, February 2, 2018.

Donald B. Redford. "The Monotheism of Akhenaten." Bible Odyssey
[Online] Available https://www.bibleodyssey.org/en/places/
related-articles/monotheism-of-akhenaten.

"Dr. Alexa Irene Canady." U.S. National Library of Medicine.
[Online] Available https://cfmedicine.nlm.nih.gov/physicians/

biography_53.html, October 14, 2003.

"Dr. Alexander T. Augusta: Patriot, Officer, Doctor." *Binding Wounds, Pushing Boundaries: African Americans in Civil War Medicine.* U.S. Department of Health & Human Services [Online] Available https://www.nlm.nih.gov/exhibition/bindingwounds/pdfs/ BioAugustaOB571.pdf.

"Dr. Eliza Ann Grier." U.S. National Library of Medicine. [Online] Available https://cfmedicine.nlm.nih.gov/physicians/ biography_132.html, October 14, 2003.

"Dr. Helen Octavia Dickens." Changing the Face of Medicine. U.S. National Library of Medicine [Online] Available https://cfmedicine. nlm.nih.gov/physicians/biography_82.html.

Dr. Howard Markel. "Celebrating Rebecca Lee Crumpler, first African-American woman physician." *PBS News Hour.* PBS [Online] Available https://www.pbs.org/newshour/health/celebrating- rebecca-lee-crumpler-first-african-american-physician, March 9, 2016.

"Dr. M. Joycelyn Elders." Changing the Face of Medicine. U.S. National Library of Medicine [Online] Available https://cfmedicine.nlm.nih. gov/physicians/biography_98.html.

"Dr. Patricia E. Bath." Changing the Face of Medicine. U.S. National Library of Medicine [Online] Available https://cfmedicine.nlm.nih. gov/physicians/biography_26.html.

"Dr. Rebecca J. Cole." U.S. National Library of Medicine. [Online] Available https://cfmedicine.nlm.nih.gov/physicians/ biography_66.html, October 14, 2003.

"Dr. Rebecca Lee Crumpler." Changing the Face of Medicine. U.S. National Library of Medicine [Online] Available https://cfmedicine. nlm.nih.gov/physicians/biography_73.html.

Dream Caszzaniga. "Remembering Donyale Luna, The African- American Model Who Transformed The Face Of Fashion." Vogue UK [Online] Available https://www.vogue.co.uk/article/donyale-luna- model-vogue, April 19, 2019.

"Dred Scott v. Sandford." Oyez [Online] Available https://www.oyez. org/cases/1850-1900/60us393.

Ed Decker. "Smith, Clarence O. 1933-." *Contemporary Black Biography.* Encyclopedia.com [Online] Available https://www.encyclopedia.com/education/news-wires-white-papers-and-books/smith-clarence-o-1933, 2005.

Ed Kopp. "A Brief History Of The Blues." All About Jazz [Online] Available https://www.allaboutjazz.com/a-brief-history-of-the-blues-by-ed-kopp.php, August 16, 2005.

Elissa Ely. "Dr. Chester Pierce Understood Racism On Multiple Fronts." WBUR [Online] Available https://www.wbur.org/remembrance-project/2017/02/08/dr-chester-pierce, February 8, 2017.

Elizabeth Engel. "Annie Turnbo Malone (1869-1957)." The State Historical Society of Missouri [Online] Available https://historicmissourians.shsmo.org/historicmissourians/name/m/malone/.

"Elizabeth Keckley." Virginia Museum of History & Culture. [Online] Available https://www.virginiahistory.org/collections-and-resources/virginia-history-explorer/elizabeth-keckley.

Elizabeth Nix. "Tuskegee Experiment: The Infamous Syphilis Study." History [Online] Available https://www.history.com/news/the-infamous-40-year-tuskegee-study, May 16, 2017.

Elizabeth Ofosuah Johnson. "Amanirenas, the brave one-eyed African queen who led an army against the Romans in 24BC. Face2FaceAfrica [Online] Available https://face2faceafrica.com/article/amanirenas-the-brave-one-eyed-african-queen-who-led-an-army-against-the-romans-in-24bc, July 17, 2018.

Elliot Partin. "Freedom's Journal (1827-1829)." BlackPast [Online] Available https://www.blackpast.org/african-american-history/freedom-s-journal-1827-1829/, January 4, 2011.

Erica L. Taylor. "Little Known Black History Fact: Black is Beautiful." Black America Web [Online] Available https://blackamericaweb.com/2013/11/26/little-known-black-history-fact-black-is-beautiful/, November 26, 2013.

Erika Weber. "Marjorie Stewart Joyner (1896-1994)." BlackPast [Online] Available https://www.blackpast.org/african-american-history/joyner-marjorie-stewart-1896-1994/, March 9, 2018.

Erin Blakemore. "How Dolls Helped Win Brown v. Board of Education." History [Online] Available https://www.history.com/news/brown-v-board-of-education-doll-experiment, March 27, 2018.

Erin Blakemore. "How the Black Power Protest at the 1968 Olympics Killed Careers." History [Online] Available https://www.history.com/news/1968-mexico-city-olympics-black-power-protest-backlash, February 22, 2018.

Erin Blakemore. "The Shocking Photo of 'Whipped Peter' That Made Slavery's Brutality Impossible to Deny." [Online] Available https://www.history.com/news/whipped-peter-slavery-photo-scourged-back-real-story-civil-war, February 7, 2019.

Errol I. Mars. "Clarence O. Smith." Black Entrepreneurs & Executives [Online] Available https://www.blackentrepreneurprofile.com/people/person/clarence-o-smith, March 18, 2004.

"Ernie Davis." Heisman Trophy [Online] Available https://www.heisman.com/heisman-winners/ernie-davis/.

Faith Cummings. "This Iconic Brand Is Back at Sephora Starting Today." Allure [Online] Available https://www.allure.com/story/madam-cj-walker-sephora, March 4, 2016.

Faithully Magazine Editors. "Alexander Archer Emancipated Himself, So Why Is He Kneeling Before Lincoln?" *Faithfully* Magazine [Online] Available https://faithfullymagazine.com/alexander-archer-emancipation-lincoln/, 2018.

Frances H. Casstevens. *The Civil War and Yadkin County, North Carolina: A History.* Jefferson, NC; McFarland & Company Inc., Publishers, 1997, p. 188.

Fred Williams. "Black Wall Street: A Legacy of Success." Ebony [Online] Available https://www.ebony.com/black-history/black-wall-street-a-legacy-of-success-798/, February 24, 2014.

"Frederick McKinley Jones, innovator of many devices." African American Registry. [Online] Available https://aaregistry.org/story/frederick-mckinley-jones-innovator-of-many-devices/.

"From Sierra Leone to the Streets of New York: The Story of Shea Moisture." Target Corporate [Online] Available https://corporate.target.com/article/2012/10/from-sierra-leone-to-the-streets-of-new-york-local, October 1, 2012.

"From slave to entrepreneur, Biddy Mason." African American Registry. [Online] Available https://aaregistry.org/story/from-slavery-to-entrepreneur-biddy-mason/.

Gaius Chamberlain. "Lewis Latimer." The Black Inventor Online Museum. [Online] Available https://blackinventor.com/lewis-latimer/, March 23, 2012.

"Garrett A. Morgan." Ohio History Central [Online] Available http://www.ohiohistorycentral.org/w/Garrett_A._Morgan.

"Garrett Augustus Morgan." PBS. [Online] Available http://www.pbs.org/wgbh/theymadeamerica/whomade/morgan_hi.html.

"Gee's Bend Quiltmakers." Souls Grown Deep [Online] Available http://www.soulsgrowndeep.org/gees-bend-quiltmakers.

Greg Prato. "Sylvester." AllMusic [Online] Available https://www.allmusic.com/artist/sylvester-mn0000756291/biography.

"Gwen Ifill Biography." The Historymakers [Online] Available https://www.thehistorymakers.org/biography/gwen-ifill-6.

"Hank Aaron." National Baseball Hall of Fame [Online] Available https://baseballhall.org/hall-of-famers/aaron-hank.

"HBCU Climate Change Consortium." Deep South Center for Environmental Justice [Online] Available http://www.dscej.org/our-work/hbcu-climate-change-consortium.

"History of Estavanico." The Estevanico Society. [Online] Available https://www.humanities.uci.edu/mclark/HumCore2001/Spring%20Quarter/Estevanico.htm.

"History of the U.S. and Morocco." U.S. Embassy & Consulate in Morocco [Online] Available https://ma.usembassy.gov/our-relationship/policy-history/io/.

"History." National Medical Association [Online] Available https://www.nmanet.org/page/History.

History.com Editors. "1937: Blues Singer Bessie Smith, killed in Mississippi car wreck, is buried." History [Online] Available https://www.history.com/this-day-in-history/blues-singer-bessie-smith-

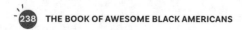

killed-in-mississippi-car-wreck-is-buried, November 13, 2009.

History.com Editors. "1955: Emmett Till is murdered." History [Online] Available https://www.history.com/this-day-in-history/the-death-of-emmett-till, February 9, 2010.

History.com Editors. "Birmingham Church Bombing." History [Online] Available https://www.history.com/topics/1960s/birmingham-church-bombing, January 27, 2010.

History.com Editors. "Buffalo Soldiers." History [Online] Available https://www.history.com/topics/westward-expansion/buffalo-soldiers, December 7, 2017.

History.com editors. "Dred Scott Decision." History. [Online] https://www.history.com/topics/black-history/dred-scott-case, Oct. 27, 2009.

History.com Editors. "Medgar Evers." History [Online] Available https://www.history.com/topics/black-history/medgar-evers, November 9, 2009.

History.com Editors. "Muhammad Ali." History [Online] Available https://www.history.com/topics/black-history/muhammad-ali, December 16, 2009.

History.com Editors. "Myrlie Evers-Williams." History [Online] Available https://www.history.com/topics/black-history/myrlie-evers-williams, December 2, 2009.

"Humble Beginnings." Nubian Heritage [Online] Available https://www.nubianheritage.com/our-story.html.

"Ibrahim Abdul-Matin." International Living Future Institute [Online] Available https://living-future.org/people/ibrahim-abdul-matin/.

"J. Strickland." CosmoBiz [Online] Available http://cosmobiz.com/en/index.php/extra/48-who-is-who/personal-care/158-j-strickland.html, December 8, 2013.

Jada Yuan and Aaron Wong. "The FIrst Black Trans Model Had Her Face on a Box of Clairol." The Cut [Online] Available https://www.thecut.com/2015/12/tracey-africa-transgender-model-c-v-r.html, December 14, 2015.

Jay Coen Gilbert. "The Coolest Deal Term Ever: Sundial Pays It

Forward." Forbes [Online] Available https://www.forbes.com/sites/
jaycoengilbert/2017/12/04/the-coolest-deal-term-ever-sundial-
pays-it-forward/#3c9622856622, December 4, 2017.

"Jeaninne Kayembe." Philadelphia Assembled. Philadelphia Museum
of Art [Online] Available http://phlassembled.net/sovereignty/
index/jeaninne_kayembe/.

"Jeaninne Kayembe: Co-Founder, Co-Executive Director, Director of
Arts & Events." Philly Urban Creators [Online] Available http://www.
phillyurbancreators.org/jeaninne-kayembe-bio.

Jeff Miller. "Harvard's Chester Pierce was trailblazer in his field
and on the field." The Undefeated [Online] Available https://
theundefeated.com/features/harvards-chester-pierce-was-
trailblazer-in-his-field-and-on-the-field/, September 29, 2016.

Jerry Portwood. "Jackie Shane, Soul Singer and Transgender Pioneer,
Dead at 78." Rolling Stone [Online] Available https://www.
rollingstone.com/music/music-news/jackie-shane-soul-singer-
transgender-obituary-798820/, February 22, 2019.

Jessica Diaz-Hurtado. "Forebears: Sister Rosetta Tharpe, The
Godmother OF Rock 'N' Roll." [Online] Available https://www.npr.
org/2017/08/24/544226085/forebears-sister-rosetta-tharpe-
the-godmother-of-rock-n-roll, August 24, 2017.

"Jim Brown." Pro Football Hall of Fame [Online] Available https://
www.profootballhof.com/players/jim-brown/.

Jimmy Fenison. "Alexander T. Augusta (1850-1890)." BlackPast
[Online] Available https://www.blackpast.org/african-american-
history/augusta-alexander-t-1825-1890/, March 29, 2009.

"Jimmie Lee Jackson." Southern Poverty Law Center [Online]
Available https://www.splcenter.org/jimmie-lee-jackson.

"Jimmie Lee Jackson: The Murder that Sparked the Selma to
Montgomery Marches of 1965." National Underground Railroad
Freedom Center [Online] Available https://freedomcenter.org/
voice/death-sparked-selma-montgomery-marches-1965.

Joan Paulson Gage. "A Slave Named Gordon." The New York Times
[Online] Available https://www.nytimes.com/2009/10/04/books
/review/Letters-t-ASLAVENAMEDG_LETTERS.html?mtrref=www.

googlecom&gwh=B9970E3463E31D60BDEAF986986D15C7&gwt=
pay&assetType=REGIWALL, September 30, 2009.

Joel Bresler. "A Cultural History." *Follow The Drinking Gourd*: A Cultural
History [Online] Available http://www.followthedrinkinggourd.org/,
2008.

"John H. Johnson Biography." The Historymakers [Online] Available
https://www.thehistorymakers.org/biography/john-h-johnson-40.

John M. Logsdon. "Guion Bluford." *Encyclopaedia Britannica* [Online]
Available https://www.britannica.com/biography/Guion-Bluford,
November 29, 2004.

Jon Swan. "The Slave Who Sued For Freedom." *American Heritage,*
Volume 41, Issue 2 [Online] (Volume 41, issue 2, 1990) https://www.
americanheritage.com/slave-who-sued-freedom, 1990.

Julianna Tesfu. "Mansa Musa (1280-1337)." BlackPast. [Online]
Available https://www.blackpast.org/global-african-history/musa-
mansa-1280-1337/, June 14, 2008.

"Jupiter Hammon." Poetry Foundation. [Online] Available https://
www.poetryfoundation.org/poets/jupiter-hammon.

Karen Ruffle. "George F. Bragg (George Freeman), 1863-1940."
Documenting the American South. [Online] Available https://
docsouth.unc.edu/church/bragg/bio.html.

Karen Sparks. "Lester Holt." Encylopaedia Britannica [Online]
Available https://www.britannica.com/topic/Lester-Holt.

"Kari Fulton." Green For All [Online] Available https://www.greenforall.
org/kari_fulton.

Kate Kelly. "Marjorie Stewart Joyner (1896-1994): Inventor of a
Permanent Hair-Wave Machine." America Comes Alive [Online]
Available https://americacomesalive.com/2014/02/17/marjorie-
stewart-joyner-1896-1994-inventor-permanent-hair-wave-
machine/, February 17, 2014.

Kate Kelly. "Mary Ellen Pleasant, Entrepreneur and Abolitionist."
America Comes Alive [Online] Available https://
americacomesalive.com/2019/02/25/mary-ellen-pleasant-
entrepreneur-and-abolitionist/, February 25, 2019.

Kathleen Cairns. "John Russwurm (1799-1851)." BlackPast [Online] Avaiable https://www.blackpast.org/african-american-history/russwurm-john-1799-1851/, January 27, 2007.

Kenan Heise. "Hair Care Founder Fred Luster." Chicago Tribune [Online] Available https://www.chicagotribune.com/news/ct-xpm-1991-03-14-9101230430-story.html, March 14, 1991.

Kerri Lee Alexander. "Elizabeth Freeman." National Women's History Museum [Online] Available https://www.womenshistory.org/education-resources/biographies/elizabeth-freeman, 2019.

"Kimberly Lewis: Senior Vice President, Market Transformation and Development, North America, U.S. Green Building Council." U.S. Green Building Council [Online] Available https://www.usgbc.org/people/kimberly-lewis/0000029816.

Kiah McBride. "Melissa Butler Went From 'Shark Tank' Rejection To The Shelves Of Major Retailers." XONecole [Online] Available https://www.xonecole.com/how-the-lip-bar-founder-went-from-shark-tank-rejection-to-a-400000-brand/, March 11, 2019.

Kim Gilmore. "The Birmingham Crusade." Biography [Online] Available https://www.biography.com/news/black-history-birmingham-childrens-crusade-1963-video, February 14, 2014.

Kimberly Nash. "The Forgotten Olympian: The Story of John Taylor." Bleacher Report [Online] Available https://bleacherreport.com/articles/171264-the-forgotten-olympian-the-story-of-john-taylor, May 9, 2009.

Lakshmi Gandhi. "The Extraordinary Story of Why A 'Cakewalk' Wasn't Always Easy." NPR CodeSwitch. [Online] Available https://www.npr.org/sections/codeswitch/2013/12/23/256566647/the-extraordinary-story-of-why-a-cakewalk-wasnt-always-easy, December 23, 2013.

Larry Nager. "W.C. Handy." Memphis Music Hall of Fame [Online] Available http://memphismusichalloffame.com/inductee/wchandy/.

"Leading With Intentionality." Harvard Business School [Online] Available https://www.exed.hbs.edu/testimonials/owner-president-management-richelieu-dennis.

Lebo Matshego. "Great Ancient African Queens." Africa.com [Online] Available https://www.africa.com/great-ancient-african-queens/, June 20, 2019.

"Lewis Latimer." Scholastic Teacher's Activity Guide [Online] Available.

http://teacher.scholastic.com/activities/bhistory/inventors/latimer. htm.

"Ma Rainey." Rock & Roll Hall of Fame [Online] Available https://www. rockhall.com/inductees/ma-rainey.

"Maggie L. Walker." National Park Service. [Online] Available https:// www.nps.gov/articles/maggie-l-walker.htm.

"Maggie L. Walker, business pioneer." African American Registry. [Online] Available https://aaregistry.org/story/maggie-l-walker-business-pioneer/.

Maggie MacClean. "Biddy Mason." History of American Women. [Online] Available http://www.womenhistoryblog.com/2013/05/ biddy-mason.html.

Maggie MacClean. "Clara Brown." History of American Women. [Online] Available http://www.womenhistoryblog.com/2015/03/ clara-brown.html.

Margot Lee Shetterly. "Dorothy Vaughan Biography." NASA [Online] Available https://www.nasa.gov/content/dorothy-vaughan-biography, August 3. 2017.

Margot Lee Shetterly. "Katherine Johnson Biography." NASA [Online] Available https://www.nasa.gov/content/katherine-johnson-biography, Aug. 16, 2018.

Marian Halley. "Mary Ellen Pleasant." Guidelines: Newsletter for San Francisco City Guides and Sponsors [Online] Available http://www.sfcityguides.org/public_ guidelines.html?article=1305&submitted=TRUE&srch_ text=&submitted2=&topic=

"Marshall 'Major' Taylor: The incredible story of the first African-American world champion." National Museum of American History [Online] Available https://americanhistory.si.edu/blog/2014/03/

marshall-major-taylor-the-incredible-story-of-the-first-african-american-world-champion.html, March 19, 2014.

Martin Iversen Christensen. "Heads of State of Sudan/Al-Jmhuryat es-Sudan." Worldwide Guide To Women In Leadership. [Online] Available https://guide2womenleaders.com/Sudan_Heads.htm.

Maryland Public Television. "Music." Pathways to Freedom: Maryland & the Underground Railroad [Online] Available https://pathways.thinkport.org/secrets/music2.cfm.

"Meet Our Founder Rue Mapp." Outdoor Afro [Online] Available https://outdoorafro.com/team/.

Melissa Butler. "My Story: Why I Started The Lip Bar." The Lip Bar [Online] Available https://www.thelipbar.com/pages/my-story?gclid=Cj0KCQjwjMfoBRDDARIsAMUjNZo_vnoN87u_S7MmY0hUIiHLJAHN8h4eaLKZz5f6dw3iwrzevHkM-IcaAliSEALw_wcB.

Melkorka Licea. "This history-making Olympian lost everything—even her medal." *New York Post* [Online] Available https://nypost.com/2018/02/17/this-history-making-olympian-lost-everything-even-her-medal/, February 17, 2018.

Melvin I. Urofsky. "Dred Scott decision."*Encyclopaedia Britannica* [Online] Available 1998. https://www.britannica.com/event/Dred-Scott-decision, July 20, 1998.

Michael Walsh. "A Year of Hope for Joplin and Johnson." *Smithsonian* Magazine [Online] Available https://www.smithsonianmag.com/history/a-year-of-hope-for-joplin-and-johnson-123024/, June 2010.

Michelle Moore. "Celebrating Black 'Green' History." Groundswell [Online] Available https://groundswell.org/celebrating-black-green-history/, February 28, 2017.

Mike D. Smith. "Birmingham's civil rights Foot Soldiers to be honored during Magic City parade, game." [Online] Available https://www.al.com/news/birmingham/2014/10/birminghams_civil_rights_foot.html, October 23, 2014.

Mitchell Willetts. "Historic Vernon AME Church in north Tulsa added to National Register." [Online] Available https://www.tulsaworld.com/news/local/historic-vernon-ame-church-in-north-

tulsa-added-to-national/article_a9d3f274-1307-5146-a6b5-
46aae7e9f869.html, September 2, 2018.

Monica White. "Food Justice Requires Land Justice: A Conversation
with Savi Horne." Edge Effects [Online] Available http://
edgeeffects.net/savi-horne/, December 12, 2017

Nancy Goldstein. *Jackie Ormes: The First African American Woman
Cartoonist* [Online] Available https://www.jackieormes.com/.

NASA Archives. "Space History Photo: Nichelle Nichols, NASA
Recruiter." Space.com [Online] Available https://www.space.
com/24147-nichelle-nichols-nasa-recruiter.html, January 3, 2014.

Natasha S. Robinson. "Betty And Coretta: An Untold Story Of
Friendship And Activism." UrbanFaith [Online] Available https://
urbanfaith.com/2013/02/betty-and-coretta-an-untold-story-of-
friendship-and-activism.html/, 2013.

National Park Service. "Bridget 'Biddy' Mason." National Park Service.
[Online] Available https://www.nps.gov/people/biddymason.htm.

NBA.com Staff. "Legends profile: Bill Russell." NBA [Online] Available
https://www.nba.com/history/legends/profiles/bill-russell.

NBA.com Staff. "Legends profile: Wilt Chamberlain." NBA [Online]
Available https://www.nba.com/history/legends/profiles/wilt-
chamberlain.

Nick Douglas. "I'm Richelieu Dennis, Owner of Essence and Sundial
Brands, and This Is How I Work." Lifehacker [Online] Available
https://lifehacker.com/im-richelieu-dennis-owner-of-essence-
and-sundial-brand-1826418739, August 29, 2018.

Octavio Blanco. "Bringing solar power and jobs to low-income
neighborhoods." CNN [Online] Available https://money.cnn.
com/2016/04/01/news/economy/solar-wdc-mark-davis/index.
html, April 1, 2016.

Olga Bourlin. "Donyale Lune (1946-1979)." BlackPast [Online] Available
https://www.blackpast.org/african-american-history/luna-
donyale-1946-1979/, June 30, 2014.

"Omar—Founder & Coordinator." Green Worker Cooperatives [Online]
http://www.greenworker.coop/omar_freilla.

"Omar Freilla." Environmental Leadership Program [Online] Available https://elpnet.org/users/omar-freilla.

Omar ibn Said. " 'Oh ye Americans': The Autobiography of Omar ibn Said, an enslaved Muslim in the United States." National Humanities Center Resource Toolbox: The Making of African American Identity: Vol I, 1500-1865 [Online] Available http://nationalhumanitiescenter.org/pds/maai/community/text3/religionomaribnsaid.pdf, 2009.

"Omar Ibn Said Collection" Library of Congress. [Online] Available https://www.loc.gov/collections/omar-ibn-said-collection/about-this-collection/.

"Our Story." Mixed Chicks. Facebook [Online] Available https://www.facebook.com/pg/MixedChicksHairCare/about/?ref=page_internal.

"Our Story." Shea Moisture [Online] Available https://www.sheamoisture.com/our-story.html.

"Overview." The Legacy of Henrietta Lacks. Johns Hopkins Medicine [Online] Available https://www.hopkinsmedicine.org/henriettalacks/index.html.

"O.W. Gurley: 'The Visionary Builder.' " Black Wall Street USA. [Online] Available http://www.blackwallstreet.org/owgurly.

Pascal-Emmanuel Gobry. "Check Out All The Businesses Jay-Z Is Into." Business Insider. [Online] Available https://www.businessinsider.com/check-out-all-the-businesses-jay-z-is-into-2010-10, October 28, 2010.

"Patrice A. Harris, MD, MA." American Medical Association [Online] Available https://www.ama-assn.org/about/board-trustees/patrice-harris-md-ma.

Patrice Grell Yursik. "Beauty Brand History-Blue Magic. Still Blue. Still Magical." Afrobella. [Online] Available https://www.afrobella.com/2014/06/03/beauty-brand-history-blue-magic/, June 3, 2014.

Paul Mohai, David Pellow and J. Timmons Roberts. "Environmental Justice." *Annual Review of Environment and Resources.* Palo Alto, CA: Annual Reviews, 2009. 34:1, pp. 405-430.

"Peggy Shepard." We Act For Environmental Justice. [Online] Available https://www.weact.org/person/peggy-shepard/.

"Peggy Shepard." Womenstrong International [Online] Available https://www.womenstrong.org/people/peggy-shepard.

"Pleasant's Story." Mary Ellen Pleasant: Mother of Civil Rights in California [Online] Available http://www.mepleasant.com/story2.html.

Raymond Arsenault. "How Arthur Ashe Transformed Tennis—and Athlete Activism." History [Online] Available https://www.history.com/news/arthur-ashe-black-tennis-champion-us-open-activism-courage, September 10, 2018.

Rebecca Skloot. *The Immortal Life of Henrietta Lacks.* New York City, NY: Random House, 2010.

"Reconstruction Era: 1865-1877." Howard University Library System [Online] Available https://www.howard.edu/library/reference/guides/reconstructionera/

Rhiannon Walker. "Ernie Davis becomes the first African-American to win the Heisman Trophy." The Undefeated [Online] Available December 7, 2016.

Rick Karr. "Bigger Than Disco, 'You Make Me Feel (Mighty Real)' Is A Celebration Of Self." NPR [Online] Available https://www.allmusic.com/artist/sylvester-mn0000756291/biography, October 8, 2018.

Robert Bullard. "The Legacy of American Apartheid and Environmental Racism." *Journal of Civil Rights and Economic Development.* Queens, NY: St. John's University School of Law, 1994.

Robert Stirling. "Samuel Eli Cornish (1795-1858)." BlackPast [Online] Available https://www.blackpast.org/african-american-history/cornish-samuel-eli-1795-1858/, December 30, 2008.

Robin Walker. "Queen Amina & Queen Bakwa Turunku." When We Ruled [Online] Available http://www.whenweruled.com/?p=84.

"Rose Brewer—Teaching Award Statement." American Sociological Association [Online] Available https://www.asanet.org/news-and-events/member-awards/distinguished-contributions-teaching-asa-award/rose-brewer-teaching-award-statement.

Ryan Velez. "Meet The Only Black Female Bank Owner In The United States." Your Black World [Online] Available http://yourblackworld. net/2018/03/29/meet-the-only-black-female-bank-owner-in-the-united-states/, March 29, 2018.

Sam Dean. "John Carlos: My Black Power salute at Mexico Olympics is as pertinent now as it was in 1968." The Telegraph [Online] Available https://www.telegraph.co.uk/olympics/2016/08/18/john-carlos-my-black-power-salute-at-mexico-olympics-is-as-perti/, August 18, 2016.

"Sam Grant: Co-chair of the Board of Directors." Sierra Leone Foundation for New Democracy [Online] Available https://www.slfnd.org/sam-grant.

Samantha Callender. "Queen Latifah Reflects On Getting Rid of the 'Ashy Stuff' For Her CoverGirl Queen Collection." *Essence* [Online] Available https://www.essence.com/beauty/makeup/queen-latifah-covergirl-queen-collection/, July 21, 2017.

Samantha Elliott Briggs. "Foot Soldiers for Justice." Birmingham Civil Rights Institute [Online] Available https://www.bcri.org/wp-content/uploads/2017/10/Foot-soldiers-lessons-and-standards.pdf, August 1, 2016.

Samuel Momodu. "Naomi Ruth Sims (1948-2009)." BlackPast [Online] Available https://www.blackpast.org/african-american-history/sims-naomi-ruth-1948-2009/, July 15, 2017.

"San Francisco's finest, Mary Ellen Pleasant." African American Registry. [Online] Available https://aaregistry.org/story/san-franciscos-finest-mary-ellen-pleasant/.

"Satchel Paige." National Baseball Hall of Fame [Online] Available https://baseballhall.org/hall-of-famers/paige-satchel.

"Savi Horne (Executive Director of the Land Loss Prevention Project), 'Agriculture, Land, and Equity' (Pierson College Tea)." Environmental Humanities. Yale University [Online] https://environmentalhumanities.yale.edu/event/savi-horne-executive-director-land-loss-prevention-project-agriculture-land-and-equity-pierson, 2019.

"Shelton Johnson." *The National Parks: America's Best Idea.* PBS [Online] http://www.pbs.org/nationalparks/people/nps/johnson/.

"Sister Rosetta Tharpe." Rock & Roll Hall of Fame [Online] Available https://www.rockhall.com/nominee/sister-rosetta-tharpe.

Sierra Leone Foundation For New Democracy [Online] Available https://www.slfnd.org/purpose.

Sondra A. O'Neale. "Phillis Wheatley." Poetry Foundation [Online] Available https://www.poetryfoundation.org/poets/phillis-wheatley.

"Songs." Negro Spirituals [Online] Available http://www.negrospirituals.com/index.html.

Stevenson Swanson and Joseph A. Kirby. "Betty Shabazz, Widow Of Malcolm X." Chicago Tribune [Online] Available https://www.chicagotribune.com/news/ct-xpm-1997-06-24-9706240184-story.html, June 24, 1997.

"Story of Us: History & Staff Bios." Philly Urban Creators [Online] Available http://www.phillyurbancreators.org/story.

"Summary of *The Story of Archer Alexander: From Slavery to Freedom.*" Documenting the American South. [Online] Available https://docsouth.unc.edu/neh/eliot/summary.html.

Susan Griffith. "Archer Alexander (CA. 1810-1879). BlackPast. [Online] Available https://www.blackpast.org/african-american-history/alexander-archer-ca-1810-1879/, April 1, 2012.

Suzanne Gould. "Why We're Still Talking about the Doll Racism Test." The American Association of University Women [Online] https://www.aauw.org/2016/02/10/doll-racism-test-today/, February 10, 2016.

"Tamron Hall." MSNBC [Online] Available http://www.msnbc.com/newsnation-tamron-hall/tamron-hall-biography.

"Tanya Fields." Green For All [Online] Available https://www.greenforall.org/tanya_fields.

"Tanya Fields." Speak Out Now [Online] Available https://www.speakoutnow.org/speaker/fields-tanya.

Teaching Tolerance Staff. "Jimmie Lee Jackson." *Free At Last: A History of the Civil Rights Movement and Those Who Died in the Struggle* [Online] Available https://www.tolerance.org/classroom-resources/texts/jimmie-lee-jackson, 1989.

Thad Morgan. "Why MLK's Right-Hand Man, Bayard Rustin, Was Nearly Written Out of History." History [Online] Available https://www.history.com/news/bayard-rustin-march-on-washington-openly-gay-mlk, June 1, 2018.

The Editors of *Encyclopaedia Britannica.* "Betty Shabazz: American Educator And Activist." *Enclyclopaedia Britannica* [Online] Available https://www.britannica.com/biography/Betty-Shabazz, December 03, 2004.

The Editors of *Encyclopaedia Britannica.* "Octavia E. Butler." *Encyclopaedia Britannica* [Online] Available https://www.britannica.com/biography/Octavia-E-Butler, July 20, 1998.

The Editors of *Encyclopaedia Britannica.* "Richard Wright." *Encyclopaedia Britannica* [Online] Available https://www.britannica.com/biography/Richard-Wright-American-writer, May 4, 1999.

The Editors of Encyclopaedia Brittanica. "Janet Collins." Encyclopaedia Brittanica [Online] Available https://www.britannica.com/biography/Janet-Collins.

The Editors of *Encylopaedia Britannica.* "Toni Morrison." *Encyclopaedia Britannica* [Online] Available https://www.britannica.com/biography/Toni-Morrison, July 20, 1998.

"The Importance of HeLa Cells." The Legacy of Henrietta Lacks. Johns Hopkins Medicine [Online] Available https://www.hopkinsmedicine.org/henriettalacks/importance-of-hela-cells.html.

"The Life of Paul Jennings." James Madison's Montpelier [Online] Available https://www.montpelier.org/learn/paul-jennings.

"The Making Of A Titan: Biography." Reginaldflewis.com [Online] Available https://reginaldflewis.com/bio/

The Official Website of Zora Neale Hurston. [Online] Available https://www.zoranealehurston.com/.

"The Race Riot That Destroyed Black Wall Street." Official Black Wall Street [Online] Available https://officialblackwallstreet.com/black-wall-street-story/, July 22, 2015.

"The Significance Of 'The Doll Test.' " NAACP Legal Defense Fund [Online] Available https://www.naacpldf.org/ldf-celebrates-60th-anniversary-brown-v-board-education/significance-doll-test/.

"The Story Behind A Statue." *The Washington Post* [online] Available https://www.washingtonpost.com/archive/opinions/1989/04/09/the-story-behind-a-statue/1454b999-3490-4efa-b8a3-63ad49e83dd1/, April 9, 1989.

"The Tuskegee Timeline." CDC [Online] https://www.cdc.gov/tuskegee/timeline.htm.

The Undefeated Staff. "Debi Thomas: the first black athlete to win a medal in the Winter Olympics." The Undefeated [Online] Available https://theundefeated.com/whhw/debi-thomas-the-first-black-athlete-to-win-a-medal-in-the-winter-olympics/, February 14, 2018.

Time Photo. "When One Mother Defied America: The Photo That Changed the Civil Rights Movement." Time. [Online] Available https://time.com/4399793/emmett-till-civil-rights-photography/, July 10, 2016.

"Timeline: Reginald F. Lewis." PBS. [Online] Available https://www.thirteen.org/program-content/timeline-reginald-f-lewis/.

"Toni Morrison dies at 88." Penguin Random House. [Online] Available https://global.penguinrandomhouse.com/announcements/toni-morrison-dies-at-88/, August 6, 2019.

"Top Moments: Earl Lloyd, Chuck Cooper, Nat Clifton blaze new path in NBA." NBA [Online] Available https://www.nba.com/history/top-moments/1950-nba-pioneers.

Tricia Wagner. "Bridget 'Biddy' Mason (1818-1891)." BlackPast [Online] Available https://www.blackpast.org/african-american-history/mason-bridget-biddy-1818-1891/, July 12, 2007.

Tyina Steptoe. "Anna Julia Haywood Cooper (1858-1964)." BlackPast. [Online] Available https://www.blackpast.org/african-american-history/cooper-anna-julia-haywood-1858-1964/, January 29, 2007.

"UCR Offense Definitions." Uniform Crime Reporting Statistics. U.S. Department of Justice [Online] Available https://www.ucrdatatool. gov/offenses.cfm.

"Upholding the Highest Bioethical Standards." The Legacy of Henrietta Lacks. Johns Hopkins Medicine [Online] Available https://www.hopkinsmedicine.org/henriettalacks/upholding-the-highest-bioethical-standards.html.

US GenWeb Archives. "Obituary for Eliza Moore, Montgomery, Alabama." US GenWeb Archives [Online] Available http://files. usgwarchives.net/al/montgomery/obits/emoore.txt, 2002.

Veronica Chambers. "Overlooked: Mary Ellen Pleasant." New York Times [Online] Available https://www.nytimes.com/ interactive/2019/obituaries/mary-ellen-pleasant-overlooked. html, 2019.

"Volt Energy." Volt Energy [Online] Available http://www.volt-energy. com/page/volt-energy.

"Washington, Warren M. (1936–)." *World of Earth Science.* Encyclopedia. com [Online] Available https://www.encyclopedia.com/science/ encyclopedias-almanacs-transcripts-and-maps/washington-warren-m-1936, 2003.

Wesley Chenault. "Herman J. Russell (1930-2014)." New Georgia Encyclopedia [Online] Available https://www.georgiaencyclopedia. org/articles/business-economy/herman-j-russell-1930-2014, May 15, 2019.

"Who We Are." Mixed Chicks [Online] Available https://mixedchicks. net/wendi-levy-kim-etheredge/.

William L. Andrews. "Harriet A. Jacobs (Harriet Ann), 1813-1897." Documenting the American South. [Online] Available https:// docsouth.unc.edu/fpn/jacobs/bio.html.

"Willie Mays." National Baseball Hall of Fame [Online] Available https://baseballhall.org/hall-of-famers/mays-willie.

Yonaia Robinson. "Elizabeth Key Grinstead (1630-1665)." BlackPast. [Online] Available https://www.blackpast.org/african-american-history/grinstead-elizabeth-key-1630/, July 14, 2016.

THE BOOK OF

Awesome

BLACK
AMERICANS

About the Author

Monique Jones is an entertainment and pop culture writer, media critic, and TV/film reviewer. Jones has written for ShockYa, TV Equals, Racialicious, Black Girl Nerds, The Nerds of Color, Tor, *Ebony*, *Entertainment Weekly*, Zora, Mediaversity Reviews, Shadow And Act, SlashFilm, *The Offing, The Birmingham Times* and *The Miami New Times*. She also writes about pop culture and media as it relates to race, culture, and representation at JUST ADD COLOR (colorwebmag. com). She resides in Birmingham, Alabama.

Who Is an
Awesome
BLACK
AMERICAN
to You?

The Book of Awesome Black Americans features a ton of great people, but there are plenty more out there who deserve to be highlighted. So we're asking for your help!

Our dream is to create another volume—or mini-volumes—of *The Book of Awesome Black Americans* featuring even more fascinating Black Americans who have changed American and world history. Who do you feel deserves to be honored?

We are inviting you to enter your nominations at my website www.colorwebmag.com. There, you'll find a form to nominate an Awesome Black American. We encourage you to fill it out, and we'll also give you credit—so please include your name and contact information!

Thanks for participating! We know your nominations, like you, are going to be awesome!

—Monique

Mango Publishing, established in 2014, publishes an eclectic list of books by diverse authors—both new and established voices—on topics ranging from business, personal growth, women's empowerment, LGBTQ studies, health, and spirituality to history, popular culture, time management, decluttering, lifestyle, mental wellness, aging, and sustainable living. We were recently named 2019's #1 fastest growing independent publisher by *Publishers Weekly*. Our success is driven by our main goal, which is to publish high quality books that will entertain readers as well as make a positive difference in their lives.

Our readers are our most important resource; we value your input, suggestions, and ideas. We'd love to hear from you—after all, we are publishing books for you!

Please stay in touch with us and follow us at:

> Facebook: Mango Publishing
>
> Twitter: @MangoPublishing
>
> Instagram: @MangoPublishing
>
> LinkedIn: Mango Publishing
>
> Pinterest: Mango Publishing

Sign up for our newsletter at www.mangopublishinggroup.com and receive a free book!

Join us on Mango's journey to reinvent publishing, one book at a time.